Dusty Shoes, Rolled-Up Sleeves, and other . . .

# SIGNS
## *of* LIFE

### DR. DAVID JEREMIAH

**with Dr. David Jeremiah**

# CONTENTS

# ABOUT
# DR. DAVID JEREMIAH
# AND TURNING POINT

**D**r. David Jeremiah is the founder of Turning Point, a ministry committed to providing Christians with sound Bible teaching relevant to today's changing times through radio and television broadcasts, audio series, books, and rallies. Dr. Jeremiah's common-sense teaching on topics such as family, prayer, worship, angels, and biblical prophecy forms the foundation of Turning Point.

David and his wife, Donna, reside in El Cajon, California, where he serves as the senior pastor of Shadow Mountain Community Church. David and Donna have four children and ten grandchildren.

In 1982, Dr. Jeremiah brought the same solid teaching to San Diego television that he shares weekly with his congregation. Shortly thereafter, Turning Point expanded its ministry to radio. Dr. Jeremiah's inspiring messages can now be heard worldwide on radio, television, and the Internet.

Because Dr. Jeremiah desires to know his listening audience, he travels nationwide holding ministry rallies and spiritual enrichment conferences that touch the hearts and lives of many people. According to Dr. Jeremiah, "At some point in time, everyone reaches a turning point; and for every person, that moment is unique, an experience to hold onto forever. There's so much changing in today's world that sometimes it's difficult to choose the right path. Turning Point offers people an understanding of God's Word as well as the opportunity to make a difference in their lives."

Dr. Jeremiah has authored numerous books, including *Escape the Coming Night* (Revelation), *The Handwriting on the Wall* (Daniel), *Overcoming Loneliness, Grand Parenting, The Joy of Encouragement, Prayer—The Great Adventure, God in You* (Holy Spirit), *Gifts from God* (Parenting), *Jesus' Final Warning, When Your World Falls Apart, Slaying the Giants in Your Life, My Heart's Desire, Sanctuary, Life Wide Open, Searching for Heaven on Earth, The Secret of the Light, Captured by Grace, Discover Paradise, Grace Givers, Why the Nativity?, Signs of Life, The 12 Ways of Christmas, 1 Minute a Day, What in the World Is Going On?,* and *The Coming Economic Armageddon.*

# ABOUT THIS STUDY GUIDE

The purpose of this Turning Point study guide is to reinforce Dr. David Jeremiah's dynamic, in-depth teaching and to aid the reader in applying biblical truth to his or her daily life. This study guide is designed to be used in conjunction with Dr. Jeremiah's *Signs of Life* audio series, but it may also be used by itself for personal or group study.

## STRUCTURE OF THE LESSONS

Each lesson is based on one of the messages in the *Signs of Life* compact disc series and focuses on specific passages in the Bible. Each lesson is composed of the following elements:

- *Outline*

The outline at the beginning of the lesson gives a clear, concise picture of the topic being studied and provides a helpful framework for readers as they listen to Dr. Jeremiah's teaching.

- *Overview*

The overview summarizes Dr. Jeremiah's teaching on the passage being studied in the lesson. Readers should refer to the Scripture passages in their own Bibles as they study the overview. Unless otherwise indicated, Scripture verses quoted are taken from the New King James Version.

- *Application*

This section contains a variety of questions designed to help readers dig deeper into the lesson and the Scriptures, and to apply the lesson to their daily lives. For Bible study groups or Sunday school classes, these questions will provide a springboard for group discussion and interaction.

- *Did You Know?*

This section presents a fascinating fact, historical note, or insight that adds a point of interest to the preceding lesson.

# Using This Guide for Group Study

The lessons in this study guide are suitable for Sunday school classes, small-group studies, elective Bible studies, or home Bible study groups. Each person in the group should have his or her own study guide.

When possible, the study guide should be used with the corresponding compact disc series. You may wish to assign the study guide lesson as homework prior to the meeting of the group and then use the meeting time to listen to the CD and discuss the lesson.

# For Continuing Study

For a complete listing of Dr. Jeremiah's materials for personal and group study call 1-800-947-1993, go online to www.DavidJeremiah.org, or write to: Turning Point, P.O. Box 3838, San Diego, CA 92163.

Dr. Jeremiah's *Turning Point* program is currently heard or viewed around the world on radio, television, and the Internet in English. *Momento Decisivo*, the Spanish translation of Dr. Jeremiah's messages, can be heard on radio in every Spanish speaking country in the world. The television broadcast is also broadcast by satellite throughout the Middle East with Arabic subtitles.

Contact Turning Point for radio and television program times and stations in your area. Or visit our website at www.DavidJeremiah.org.

# SIGNS OF LIFE

A man named Dennis, who lived in Katy, Texas, was preparing to go out of town on a Tuesday. And as usual, he was behind schedule in his preparations. He needed to take a suit to the cleaners and get it back the same day. He remembered a dry-cleaners in his town with a big sign that said, "One-Hour Dry Cleaners." *Perfect*, he thought. So he drove across town to the establishment.

After filling out the drop-off ticket, he said, "I'll need to get this back in an hour."

The clerk said, "Sorry, but the soonest I can have it for you is Thursday."

"I thought you did dry-cleaning in an hour," Dennis said, surprised.

"No," the clerk replied, "that's just the name of the store."

A one-hour dry cleaners that doesn't do dry-cleaning in an hour? How confusing is that? Probably just as confusing as Christians who claim to be Christians but fail to act like the One whose name they bear.

Imagine a professing Christian screaming and shouting obscenities and shaking his fist at someone who cuts him off in traffic. "I thought you were a Christian," his car-pool companion says. "Oh, no," the driver responds, "that's just what I tell people at work. It's just a label I use to make people think I'm a nice person."

Can you imagine? It's only right for people to expect those who follow Jesus Christ to bear some resemblance to Him and to obey His teachings. As someone has said, "If you're gonna wear the name, you need to act the same."

What are the signs that a person who claims to be a Christian is a true follower of Jesus Christ? There are many, of course, but a good example is one Jesus gave directly to His twelve disciples. "By this all will know that you are My disciples, if you have love for one another" (John 13:35). Love, compassion, tenderness, understanding, forgiveness—because Jesus manifested those traits, so should we who claim to be His disciples.

The purpose of this study guide is to examine five categories of divine life that should be evident in every Christian. "Signs of life" they are called: Dusty Shoes (a relevant life), Worn-Out Knees (a yielded, peaceful, and submissive life), Rolled-Up Sleeves (an authentic, servant's life), Open Hands (a generous life based on God's Harvest Law), and Outstretched Arms (a compassionate, community-based life). These lifestyle traits are like signs that we hang over the door to our life that tell people what they should expect to find within. And because these were all traits that Jesus Christ manifested in His life, when people enter into a relationship with us, they gain some perspective on who Christ is.

If the church is going to make an impact in this world, it will do so only on the basis of authenticity and truthfulness. We cannot claim to be one thing with our words and then reveal we are something different by our lives. These signs of life certainly need to be practiced within the church, but they definitely need to be practiced in the Christian's neighborhood, workplace, and community as well.

*Signs of Life* can serve as a self-evaluation tool for every Christian. Each lesson's biblical theme, and the accompanying application questions, will be used by the Holy Spirit to help the reader see inconsistencies between the sign on the front of his life and the signature that warrants who he or she really is. By building the five categories of signs of life into one's walk with Christ, there'll be no inconsistency at all.

# THE FIVE SIGNS OF LIFE

*Selected Scriptures*

*In this lesson we find five characteristics of Christ
that should also characterize His followers.*

---

## OUTLINE

When a patient is brought into a hospital emergency room, he is immediately checked for "vital signs" of life. We could do the same check on the body of Christ. If we are not manifesting the same signs of life in our lives that Christ did, our world will never see Him as they should.

I. **Dusty Shoes—Living a Relevant Life**
   A. In the Life of Christ
   B. In the Lives of Christians
      1. We Have Been Sent to Be Salt
      2. We Have Been Sent to Be Light

II. **Worn-Out Knees—Living a Yielded Life**
   A. In the Life of Christ
   B. In the Lives of Christians

III. **Rolled-Up Sleeves—Living an Authentic Life**
   A. In the Life of Christ
   B. In the Lives of Christians

IV. **Open Hands—Living a Generous Life**
   A. In the Life of Christ
   B. In the Lives of Christians

V. **Outstretched Arms—Living a Compassionate Life**
   A. In the Life of Christ
   B. In the Lives of Christians

T hree souls arrived at the pearly gates of heaven and met with St. Peter. Knowing they had just arrived, and that their funerals were about to be held on earth, Peter asked each one what they hoped people would say about them at their funerals.

The first person said, "I would be most gratified to hear them say that I'd lived a useful life as a doctor and as a family man."

The second replied, "I would be happy to hear them say that I was an excellent school teacher, a wonderful wife and mother, and an asset to my community."

Everyone looked expectantly at the third person, who said without hesitation, "I would like to hear them say, 'Look! He's moving!' " Now that's a man in love with life!

Just as there should be signs of life if someone is physically alive, so there should be signs of spiritual life as well. And that is the subject of this study guide—signs of spiritual life in those who profess to be followers of the Lord Jesus Christ.

There are some signs of life that are recognized in the Christian community—signs such as worship, Bible reading, giving, the fruit of the Spirit, and others. But there should also be signs of life that are recognized outside the church—in the marketplace of this world. Jesus Christ was certainly recognized for the spiritual life that He manifested. And those that follow Him should also manifest clear signs of life.

In this introductory lesson, we're going to talk about signs of life like dusty shoes (a relevant life), worn-out knees (a prayerful life), rolled-up sleeves (a life of service), open hands (a generous life), and outstretched arms (a compassionate life). Jesus Christ had a body when He was on earth; but when He departed, the term "body of Christ" was applied to His followers. Individually and corporately, we are to demonstrate the same life in the body of Christ that Christ did through His own body while He was on earth.

# Dusty Shoes—Living a Relevant Life

Dusty shoes are a sign of someone who has left the safety of home and is out in the world, making a difference, just like Christ did.

## *In the Life of Christ (Acts 10:38)*

Jesus was a person with dusty shoes: "How God anointed Jesus of Nazareth with the Holy Spirit and with power, who went about doing good and healing all who were oppressed by the devil, for God was with Him."

Jesus wasn't ensconced in an ivory tower, a gilded palace, or ornate sanctuary—He was out in the world on the dusty roads of Israel. He "went about all Galilee" (Matthew 4:23) preaching the gospel, healing the brokenhearted, proclaiming liberty to the captives, and setting free the oppressed (Luke 4:18–19). Jesus didn't wait for people to come to Him. He put on His sandals and went out on the dusty roads to take the message of the gospel to them.

## *In the Lives of Christians (John 17:18)*

Jesus once spoke these words to the Father in prayer: "As You sent Me into the world, I also have sent [the disciples] into the world" (John 17:18). It is plain from these words that we have been sent into the world to bear the same redemptive message that Christ brought from heaven. That is, if Jesus had dusty shoes, then so should we.

Here's a helpful statement that I heard an old Baptist teacher say: "If we will be to Jesus what Jesus was to the Father, then Jesus will be to us what the Father was to Him." In other words, as the Father helped Jesus in His ministry, so Jesus will help us in ours (Mark 16:20). Jesus went into the world representing the Father, and we are to go into the world representing Jesus.

Jesus summarized under two headings what we are to be when we go into the world: salt and light.

1. We Have Been Sent to Be Salt (Matthew 5:13)

   The phrase "salt of the earth" is well-known in our culture, even among non-Christians. Today, when used to describe an individual, "salt of the earth" means a good and decent person. But what did it mean in Jesus' day?

   Those to whom Jesus spoke would have known immediately what He meant. Salt was a preservative in the days before refrigeration, especially in cultures where fish was a staple of the diet. Fish could be kept edible for many days after being caught by using salt to retard spoilage of the flesh. So when Jesus said that His followers are the salt of the earth, they knew what He meant: believers should have a "preserving" effect on the cultures of the world—we should retard the spoilage promoted by the influence of evil.

   While it's easy to feel pessimistic about the impact we're having on retarding spiritual spoilage in the world, think about what the world would be like if Christians were not present. In fact, we have a graphic picture of what that will be like by the Bible's teaching on the Great Tribulation when believers will have been removed from the world. Literally, all hell is going to break loose on planet earth. The Holy Spirit, who dwells on earth in the persons of Christ's followers, will be removed from the earth, and there will be nothing to hold back the tide of evil.

Besides being a preservative, salt also creates thirst in living beings. Jesus used the term to say we should, by our lives, make people thirsty to know the reality of God in their lives. People who don't know God should look at Christians and be attracted to the life that God makes it possible to live.

2. We Have Been Sent to Be Light (Matthew 5:14–15)

Besides salt, Jesus said His followers are light in this world, a truth that stems from the fact that Jesus first said He was the light of the world (John 8:12). But part way through His ministry, He told the disciples that "the light" would only be with them a little while (John 12:35). As long as He was in the world, Jesus said, God's light would be in the world (John 9:5). But then we have Him telling His followers that they are the light.

While Jesus was in the world, He was the light. When He left, He commissioned His disciples to take His light and spread it throughout the world. We have not become the light in the same way Jesus is the divine light. Rather, we are reflectors of His light as He lives in us through the presence of the Holy Spirit. We are to invade the spiritual darkness of this world with the light of Christ, allowing people to see truth for the first time in their lives. We are to let our "light so shine before men that they may see your good works and glorify your Father who is in heaven" (Matthew 5:16).

Being the church, the body of Christ, is about preserving and illuminating this world, pushing back evil and darkness, so that mankind might embrace the Gospel. That's what it means to have dusty shoes.

# Worn-Out Knees—Living a Yielded Life

Just as Christ was a prayerful person, so should those be who are His followers.

### In the Life of Christ (Mark 1:35)

It's important to remember that when Christ came to earth, He divested himself of His heavenly prerogatives. As a man, He had the same need to communicate with the Father as we do. He became subject to the will of His heavenly Father; and prayer was one of the ways He demonstrated His submission to, and dependence on, God.

The Gospels make frequent note of Jesus' prayer life (for example, Mark 1:35; 6:46; Luke 6:12). Luke records nine different occasions on which Jesus prayed in a variety of settings and for many different reasons. In fact, Jesus has been praying for the last 2,000 years as He makes intercession for the church (Romans 8:34; Hebrews 7:25).

### In the Lives of Christians (John 14:14)

If the Son of God needed to pray, how much more do we? Jesus said that we "ought to pray and not lose heart" (Luke 18:1). He told us to ask, seek, and knock (Matthew 7:7–8). And He warned that the spirit of man is willing, but the flesh of man is weak (Matthew 26:41). Prayer is where the real battle of the spiritual life exists, and the flesh would rather do anything except pray. In our casual, energetic culture, we have learned to pray while we jog, work out, or take walks for exercise. And that's fine. But Jesus found it necessary to get away and do nothing but pray—probably the kind of example we should follow.

# Rolled Up Sleeves—Living an Authentic Life

There was no pretense about Jesus Christ. He lived with His sleeves rolled up, as a servant, doing the work of the kingdom.

### In the Life of Christ (Matthew 20:25–28)

Jesus made it plain that He came not to lord it over people but to be a servant (Matthew 20:25–28). The ultimate expression of His service, of course, was His giving of His life to be a "ransom for many" (Mark 10:45). While we can't duplicate that act, we can follow the second greatest example of service He left us—humbling himself to wash the feet of His disciples (John 13:1–5). When we perform similar acts of humility and service, we are showing signs of the life of Christ.

### In the Lives of Christians (John 13:14)

The night He washed their feet, Jesus told His disciples that they ought to serve one another the way He was serving them (John 13:14)—another example of our being in the world to do what Jesus did. Jerry White has pointed out that it seems far more noble to us to be a servant of God than a servant of our fellow man.[1] But the way we serve God is by serving others. To claim to be a servant of God but be unwilling to serve others is to betray the shallowness of our understanding.

# OPEN HANDS—LIVING A GENEROUS LIFE

We can't talk about Jesus without talking about giving—He who gave himself for the sins of the whole world.

### In the Life of Christ (Galatians 1:4; 2:20)

In Galatians, Paul makes it clear that it was Jesus who "gave himself for our sins" (1:4) and who "loved [us] and gave himself for [us]" (2:20). It is consistent with the other paradoxes in Scripture that one of Christ's signs of life was His death. His death was a sign of life because He died willingly so that others might live—laying down His life for others (John 15:13).

### In the Lives of Christians (Acts 20:35)

If Jesus lived His life as a giver (and He did), then in order for us to manifest signs of His life in the world, we must do the same. The apostle Paul quoted words of Jesus that are not recorded in the four gospels: "It is more blessed to give than to receive" (Acts 20:35). That, of course, is contrary to the philosophy of this world that places a higher premium on receiving than on giving. Only those who have developed a lifestyle of giving know just how blessed the results of giving can be.

# Outstretched Arms—Living a Compassionate Life

Jesus was a person who felt the passion (suffering) of others—and He responded. We are to do the same.

## *In the Life of Christ (Matthew 14:14)*

Matthew 14:14 says that Jesus was "moved with compassion, and healed their sick." His compassion launched Him into action. He was moved with compassion at peoples' hunger (Matthew 15:32) and their physical afflictions (Matthew 20:34; Mark 1:40–41). Those afflicted by demonic powers were also the objects of His compassion (Mark 5:19), as well as a woman who had lost her son (Luke 7:11–15). Indeed, the masses of spiritually lost people Jesus encountered provoked compassion within Him (Matthew 9:36; Mark 6:34).

One of the lessons about signs of life to draw from Jesus is that human suffering provokes compassion in those who are spiritually alive. Christ was moved with compassion for numerous reasons as He encountered the broken lives of everyday people in His world. In a day when it was common for the poor, needy, and suffering to be overlooked, Jesus stood out because of His compassion—a sure sign that He was a teacher who had come from God (John 3:2).

## *In the Lives of Christians (Matthew 25:40)*

It is easy for us to become insulated in our own little world of provision and fail to see those around us who are hurting—people for whom Christ would have compassion. We think the government safety net systems are going to take care of them. Or we think they are irresponsible people who are just out to get what they can from gullible strangers. Those are not signs of the life of Christ in us. We should pray that we never get to the point in our life where we fail to feel for others. God is pleased when we reach out to those around us—especially those who have nothing with which to repay us—with the compassionate heart and hands of Jesus.

Jesus gave to us, had compassion on us, when we had nothing and were unable to help ourselves. And He calls on us to do the same.

As you work through this study guide, ask God to show you areas where signs of life need to be revitalized. You may be the only sign of Jesus' life some people will ever see.

Note:

1. Jerry White, *Honesty, Morality, & Conscience* (Colorado Springs: NavPress, 1979), 81–82.

1. Read Acts 10:38.

   a. When was Jesus anointed by the Holy Spirit? (Matthew 3:13–17)

   b. Following His anointing, what was the first demonstration of Jesus' power? Power to do what? (Matthew 4:1–11)

   c. What did Jesus go about "doing"? From your knowledge of the life of Christ, what kinds of things did this include? (What kinds of things in addition to miracles?)

   d. Today, what would characterize a Christian who "went about doing good"?

   e. To understand why Jesus went about "healing all who were oppressed by the devil" . . .

- How do 1 John 3:8 and 5:19 provide background?

- How do Matthew 4:17 and Colossians 1:13 help in terms of the clashing of two kingdoms?

f. How should we help those who are "oppressed by the devil" today? Is there still a need today to advance the kingdom of God into the domain of darkness?

g. We are not Christ in terms of our ability to work miracles. But how does Mark 16:20 suggest that Jesus is still willing to work through us?

h. How does the phrase "for God was with Him" tie in with John 20:21?

i. If God the Father was with Jesus, and Jesus changed the world, what does Jesus' being with us suggest about our possibilities?

2. From the following verses, note all the different places Jesus went as He preached the gospel:

a. What geographical regions? (Matthew 4:23; Mark 7:24; Luke 4:44)

b. In what religious settings? (Matthew 21:14; Luke 4:44)

c. In what social settings? (Matthew 8:14; John 2:1–2)

d. With what kinds of people? (Matthew 9:10–11; Matthew 26:6; Mark 5:38; Luke 7:36, 39)

e. What do you conclude about the example Jesus set in terms of "dusty shoes?" (How should we follow His example?)

3. List the categories Jesus used to define His ministry in Luke 4:18:

a. Preach to the _____ .

b. Heal the _____-_____ .

c. Proclaim _____ to the _____

and _____ of _____ to the

_____ .

d. To set free the _____.

e. What is the prerequisite for Jesus' being able to do all these things, geographically speaking? (He had to _____ where those in need were.)

f. How many poor, brokenhearted, captive, blind (physically or spiritually), or oppressed people have you visited recently?

g. If you are going to duplicate Jesus' ministry to these (and other) groups, what will it require on your part? What kind of "shoes?"

---

### DID YOU KNOW?

The dust Jesus got on His sandals was the dust of the Holy Land. The land area commonly referred to today as Israel was most often called Canaan in the Old Testament. Later, after the descendants of Jacob (Israel) inhabited the land, it became known as the "land of Israel," or Israel. "Palestine" came into use during the Roman era and was a "Romanized" version of the Semitic Philistia. The term "Palestine" doesn't occur in the English Bible, and Philistia occurs less than a dozen times. "Palestine" stuck as the designation for the land until 1948 when Israel was formalized as a nation, though "Palestinians" (Arabs) in the region still refer to it as Palestine.

# DUSTY SHOES—LIVING A RELEVANT LIFE

### Matthew 5:13–16

*In this lesson we learn what it
means to be salt and light in the world.*

## OUTLINE

Christians often lament that as one person, they can have little impact in the world. But even a single grain of salt can be tasted, and a single candle can dispel the darkness in a room. Jesus Christ said His followers are to be both salt and light—preserving and illuminating the world.

### I. We Are the Salt of the Earth
   A. Salt Prevents Decay
   B. Salt Provides Flavor
   C. Salt Promotes Thirst
   D. Salt Permeates Food

### II. We Are the Light of the World
   A. Light Destroys Darkness
   B. Light Detects Evil
   C. Light Discovers Good
   D. Light Defines Christianity
   E. Light Demands Exposure

A baby camel (as babies will do), was peppering his mother with questions one day about his big feet, his long eyelashes, and the big hump on his back. His mother replied that they were all to help him traverse the hot, dry, windy, sandy terrain of the desert. Then the baby camel said, "But Mom, if we were designed to survive well in the desert, why are we in the zoo?"

Good question—and one we have to ask of ourselves as followers of Jesus Christ. We have been given all the resources we need to carry out Christ's Great Commission to take the Gospel into the difficult surroundings of our world, yet we seem to spend most of our lives in the comfortable, safe confines of the church.

This raises the question, "Is Christianity social, or is it solitary?" That is, "Should I share my faith in Jesus Christ with others, or is my faith a personal thing to be kept to myself?" It appears that too many Christians have opted for the latter answer, circling the wagons to keep the "good guys" in and the "bad guys" out. Billy Graham, addressing this flaw in the church's thinking, has written, "Instead of becoming salt and light, we have been content to withdraw into our separate ecclesiastical ghettos, preoccupied with our own internal affairs and unconcerned about the deepest needs of those around us." [1]

One of the great Christians of the eighteenth century was John Wesley, one of the founders of the Methodist church. He commented on Matthew 5:13–16, saying, "I will endeavor to show that Christianity is essentially a social religion, and that to return it to a solitary religion is indeed to destroy [Christianity]." [2] John Wesley had dusty shoes, traveling all over England on horseback to preach the Gospel to those in need. And Christ has called us to be and do the same—to take the Gospel into societies around the world. To live only in our holy huddle on Sunday is to defeat the purpose for which the church has been called by Christ—to go into the world.

Jesus' words in Matthew 5:13–16 define exactly the role the Christian is to have in the world: being salt and light.

# WE ARE THE SALT OF THE EARTH
## (MATTHEW 5:13)

We touched on these words of Jesus in the previous lesson—but let's look more closely here: "You are the salt of the earth; but if the salt loses its flavor, how shall it be seasoned? It is then good for nothing but to be thrown out and trampled underfoot by men."

## Salt Prevents Decay

In Jesus' day there was no way to keep animal flesh fresh for any length of time. Salt provided the answer, either applied directly to the meat or as a saline (brine) solution. The reason salt aided preservation is that the bacteria normally responsible for the decomposition of flesh cannot exist in a highly saline environment.

Our world is like animal flesh—it is slowly decomposing in a spiritual sense due to the "bacteria" of sin. Left to itself, without outside efforts to preserve it, the world would decompose spiritually. The "salt" that God uses to preserve the world while the Gospel is being spread is the body of Christ—individual Christians being "salty" in the world.

At the end of the nineteenth century, there was a great feeling of optimism in the world. The Industrial Revolution that began in England and spread to America gave man a sense of power over his destiny. Martyn Lloyd-Jones has summarized the prevailing mood: "Wars were going to be abolished, diseases were going to be cured, suffering was going to be not only ameliorated but finally eradicated. It was to be an amazing century. Most of the problems were going to be solved, for man had at last really begun to think. The masses, through education, would cease giving themselves to drink and immorality and vice. And as all nations were thus educated to think and to hold conferences instead of rushing to war, the whole world was very soon going to be Paradise." [3]

The great World War in the early part of the twentieth century shocked mankind back to reality. Apparently man was not so civilized after all. At the beginning of the twenty-first century, no one in the world believed that mankind was headed toward Utopia. Indeed, things seem to be getting worse instead of better.

It is this "getting worse" that the church has been put in the world to delay. Our role as salt is not one of pride or "holier than thou." It is only the presence of Christ in us by the Holy Spirit that makes us a preserving agent at all. Were it not for the Spirit in us, we would be part of the degenerative process ourselves.

Christian researcher George Barna tells us that, in some ways (for example, divorce), Christians are faring no better than the world. On the other hand, who would be speaking for the unborn in our society if Christians were absent? There might be a few voices heard, but not many. So the church is definitely having an impact in many important areas. And we need to lift our voices even higher to make God's perspective on the great issues of our day known. You'll be called "politically incorrect" or worse, but it is our calling to preserve the culture so that the Gospel may spread.

## Salt Provides Flavor

Not only does salt retard decay, it provides flavor. Just as salt provides flavor to our food, so Christ in us provides flavor in an unsavory world. Life in this world without Christ can be bland and tasteless. The world may satisfy for a while, but not for long. Jesus brings a flavor to life that makes a real difference. Everything else in life can stay the same; but when one comes to know Christ, it seems as if everything changes. For that reason, there ought to be a significant difference in Christians—the world ought to be drawn to the flavor of Christ in the world like a hungry diner is drawn to salt for his food.

Because of Christ in us, everything we do should stand out. We ought to be the most faithful, the most generous, the hardest working, the most loving. In everything we do, the flavor of Jesus Christ ought to stand out in a bland world. Even in small things, like leaving tips for servers and others who depend on tips for most of their income. When servers see Christians bowing their heads to pray before a meal, then discover they leave a paltry tip— or no tip at all—how do you think that impacts the world's view of Christ? Be salty in this world! Do everything in such a way that people are drawn to the wonderful flavor of Jesus.

## Salt Promotes Thirst

When I was a small boy, I would visit my uncle and aunt on their farm in Pennsylvania. It was there that I learned about saltlicks. I'd never seen the large blocks of salt that my uncle put out for the cows to lick during the day. The cows liked the salt for the same reason we like it—because it tastes good. But when they licked the salt, it made them thirsty. And when they got thirsty, they would drink lots of water which was necessary to keep up their milk production.

So salt makes cows, and us, thirsty. And in a spiritual sense, the same is true. We are to be the salt of the earth to make people want to drink deeply of the living water that is Jesus.

In Jesus' day, during the Feast of Tabernacles in Jerusalem, the priests went to the Pool of Siloam and filled large jugs with water which was poured out on the altar of the Temple. This ritual was performed for seven days. On the seventh day, the priests went to the Pool seven times and poured out the water on the altar. On that last day, Jesus cried out to those observing this ritual saying, "If anyone thirsts, let him come to Me and drink. He who believes in Me, as the Scripture has said, out of his heart will flow rivers of living water" (John 7:37–38).

Jesus was drawing a contrast between the water of religious rituals and living water that only He could provide. And the same is true today. If people see us totally satisfied with Jesus, not drinking of the things of this world, they will want to know why. As the salt of the earth, we are to make them thirsty for Him.

Francis of Assisi once said, "Preach the Gospel at all times, and if necessary use words." His meaning was obviously in line with what we are saying in this lesson. By virtue of being salt and light, our relationship with Jesus should be evident to all and should attract others to Him. When the church is so much like the world that the world sees no difference, the Gospel suffers.

## Salt Permeates Food

The fourth thing salt does is permeate food. The reason there are such small holes in the top of the salt shaker is that a little salt goes a long way! The impact of salt is way out of proportion to its size—and so it is with Christians in this world. Sometimes Christians think, "What can I do? I'm only one person." One person may be as small as a grain of salt compared to the world, but even one grain of salt is noticeable when tasted. And history is filled with examples of individual Christians who made a world of difference.

William Wilberforce is an example. Almost single-handedly he brought an end to England's participation in the slave trade. He was small, sickly, and did not appear to be a man of any great impact. But God used him to convict the English parliament that trafficking in human slaves was wrong. And England outlawed the practice.

Most Christians I know think they couldn't possibly make a difference for Jesus. They are too busy earning a living, managing their families, and just trying to make it to church on Sunday. But we can make a difference simply by being in this world if we are living as salt and light. By our very presence, living a faithful life for Christ, the world will be preserved, made thirsty, and made hungry for Him. British political philosopher, Edmund Burke said this: "Nobody makes a greater mistake than he who did nothing because he could only do a little."

# We Are the Light of the World
## (Matthew 5:14–15)

Jesus also said, "You are the light of the world. A city that is set on a hill cannot be hidden. Nor do they light a lamp and put it under a basket, but on a lampstand, and it gives light to all who are in the house."

### Light Destroys Darkness (John 1:5)

Salt holds back evil and its destruction, but light shines forth that which is good. And we are called to be both. Ironically, it is while we are light—manifesting righteousness—that evil is held at bay. Darkness is nothing other than the absence of light. Turn off a light in a room with no windows and what happens? It is instantly dark. Turn the light back on and darkness disappears. As we shine forth the light of Christ in this world, darkness will be driven back.

### Light Detects Evil (John 3:19–20)

It is by the presence of light that deeds are illuminated. And in the case of this world, the evil deeds of the world are illuminated by the presence of Christians in the world. In other words, the light of Christ is the standard, or benchmark, for righteousness. With that standard in the world, evil deeds are contrasted and made visible. Without the light of Christ in the church, the evil deeds of the world would have nothing against which to be measured.

### Light Discovers Good (John 3:21)

When those who are responding to the light come closer to the light of Christ present in the church, their deeds become clearly visible. It becomes obvious that God is at work in their life.

### Light Defines Christianity (Ephesians 5:8)

Paul says that, though we were once darkness, we are now "light in the Lord" and should therefore "walk as children of light." The vast majority of the crime in the world takes place at night. As John wrote, "Men loved darkness rather than light, because their deeds were evil" (John 3:19). But we have been called as children of light—and light is the essence of Christianity. The darker the world around us gets, the brighter our light shines in contrast.

### Light Demands Exposure (Matthew 5:14–16)

The purpose of light is to illuminate. Jesus said we are to let our light shine so brightly "that [men] may see your good works and glorify your Father in heaven" (verse 16). If our light is concealed by the fact that we stay at home or stay at church and never let the world see our light, what is accomplished? For light to accomplish its purpose, it must leave the presence of other lights and go out into the darkness!

When salt loses its flavor, Jesus said, it is worthless. And when a light is put under a basket, it too is worthless. For the church to accomplish its purpose of preservation and illumination in the world, we must go out into the world where decay and darkness are present. Even as a solitary Christian, you can be as effective as one grain of salt and one candle—if only you will go where you are needed.

Notes:

1. Billy Graham, "Recovering the Primacy of Evangelism," *Christianity Today*, 12/8/97. http://ctlibrary.com/992.

2. John Wesley, "Sermon 24: Upon Our Lord's Sermon on the Mount, Discourse 4," 1872 ed. http://www.ccel.org/ccel/wesley/sermons.v.xxiv.html.

3. D. Martyn Lloyd-Jones, *Studies in the Sermon on the Mount* (Grand Rapids: Wm B. Eerdmans, 1967), Vol. I, 150–151.

1. Read 1 Timothy 2:1–4.

   a. Why does Paul say that prayers should be offered for "kings" and those "in authority"? (verse 2)

   b. How do "godliness and reverence" suggest "salt" and "light" discussed in this lesson? (verse 2)

   c. If there is peace in the land, and Christians are able to live godly lives, what is the desired result? (verse 4)

   d. Rather than praying for peace only as a means to avoiding conflict, what is another good reason to pray for peace and to live a godly life? (verse 4)

2. How does Colossians 4:6 illustrate the concept of salt as a "flavoring"?

   a. In what way should a Christian's speech reflect the "flavor" of the presence of Christ in his life?

   b. If our speech is not sound, what opportunity does that give to opponents of the Gospel? (Titus 2:8)

   c. What do edifying words do for those who hear? (Ephesians 4:29)

d. Conversely, what impact might corrupt words have on "the hearers"?

e. How carefully do you think non-Christians listen to what Christians say in unguarded moments?

f. Where must salt first be present in order for it to show up as flavoring in speech? (Matthew 12:34)

g. List the kinds of speech that could have a detrimental effect in terms of the Gospel (Ephesians 5:4; Colossians 3:8).

3. Read Luke 11:34–36.

   a. In what sense is the eye the "lamp of the body"?

   b. Under what circumstances is our eye "good" or "bad"?

   c. What is the implication of verse 36? Can we be partly light and partly dark? How could a Christian not be completely "full of light"?

   d. How does the Christian go about keeping his life completely filled with light? How does 1 John 1:9 fit into this process?

e. What is the best way for Christians to make sure they are continually walking in the light? (John 8:12)

4. What light does John 3:19 shed on the task of spreading the Gospel in this world? Are people going to embrace the light or resist the light?

5. What is the result of someone in darkness turning to the light? (Acts 26:18)

---

### DID YOU KNOW?

---

Modern table salt is not like the salt used in ancient cultures. Table salt today has been refined so that it is little more than pure sodium chloride. Most table salt is iodized, meaning iodine has been added for health benefits. However, ancient salt (and modern salts such as sea salt or Himalayan rock salt) is more than sodium chloride. The minerals left after evaporating ocean water contain not only sodium chloride and iodine but all the rest of the 90+ chemical elements in nature needed for human health. That makes sea salt, or natural rock salt, a healthier alternative than refined salt. Pure salt was so valuable in the ancient world that it was used as currency in many cultures.

# DUSTY SHOES—LIVING A PRODUCTIVE LIFE

## *John 15:1–8*

*In this lesson we learn what it means to bear spiritual fruit for Christ.*

### OUTLINE

In the agrarian culture of the Bible, everybody understood metaphors like fruit, vineyard, seed, soils, and harvests. When Jesus Christ said He is the vine and His followers are the branches, everyone understood what it meant: His followers' lives were to be an offshoot of His own.

I. **The Importance of Fruit-Bearing in the Bible**
   A. It Is the Mark of Your Genuine Faith
   B. It Is the Measure of Your Walk With God
   C. It Is the Motivation Behind God's Discipline
   D. It Is the Method of Touching Other People
   E. It Is the Manifestation of Christ to the World
   F. It Is the Means of Glorifying the Father

II. **The Illustrations of Fruit-Bearing in the Bible**
   A. Character
   B. Conduct
   C. Contributions
   D. Communication
   E. Converts

E verybody wants power in life. Whether it's a businessman, politician, or athlete—or any other person—everybody wants power. And that's not a bad thing. Think of how far you would get today if you discovered your car had no power. Power is ability, and it's neither good nor bad. It's what we do with the power and ability we have that matters—even in the Christian life.

The Bible tells us that Christians are connected to the greatest power source in the universe—the power of God. His power is available to help us accomplish the things we are called to do for Him. But if we don't stay connected to God's power, we live far beneath our potential.

In John 15 we have the record of part of Jesus' teachings to His disciples on the night of His arrest. They had finished the Passover meal and, many scholars believe, had left the room where they had gathered in Jerusalem before heading to the Garden of Gethsemane on the shoulders of the Mount of Olives. Perhaps they passed through vineyards along the way that sparked the words we will look at in this lesson: Jesus' words about himself as the true vine and the disciples as branches connected to Him.

Just as a branch cannot bear fruit on its own, neither can we bear fruit in the Christian life without the power that comes from being connected to the True Vine that is Jesus. But connected *to Him,* there is no limit to what we can accomplish *through Him.* Jesus is not saying we will have unlimited power to do whatever we want in life. Being connected to Jesus is not like having a genie in a bottle—power to use in a self-centered way. But He is saying that if we want to have a life of eternal significance, we have to stay connected to Him. And connected to Him, we can definitely have a life that bears fruit.

A key phrase in John 15—"without Me you can do nothing" (verse 5)—is balanced by the words of Philippians 4:13: "I can do all things through Christ who strengthens me." When it comes to spiritual power and ability in our life—the ability to bear fruit that lasts forever—Christ is the issue.

# THE IMPORTANCE OF FRUIT-BEARING IN THE BIBLE

The Bible was written in an agrarian culture, so using "fruit" as a metaphor for spiritual productivity was easy to understand. There are six reasons why it's important to understand what it means to be a fruit-bearing Christian.

### *It Is the Mark of Your Genuine Faith*

Fruitfulness is the mark of your genuine faith. Jesus said in Matthew 7:20, "Therefore by their fruits you will know them." Also, "a tree is known by its fruit" (Matthew 12:33). If a person is a Christian, there will be fruit—evidence—that indicates the life that is in him. It is possible to profess to be a follower of Jesus, like Judas Iscariot, but never produce any fruit. The lack of that fruit over time indicates the lack of any true spiritual life in that person. Jesus Christ will manifest himself in the person's life who is truly born again by the Spirit of God.

### *It Is the Measure of Your Walk With God*

The kind of fruit we produce is a measure of our walk with Christ. In John 15 there are references to "fruit" (verse 2), "more fruit" (verse 2), and "much fruit" (verse 5). In other words, there are degrees of productivity in the spiritual life—not all believers will bear the same amount of fruit. The quality and quantity of fruit we produce for the Lord should follow an upward path. As spiritual babies, we produce little fruit. But as mature saints, we should be producing "much fruit." It is helpful to look back over our life and see if our fruitfulness is increasing. Am I making progress? Like a healthy grape vine that continues to produce increasing amounts of fruit through the years, so should we. Abiding in Christ (verse 7) is the secret to increasing levels of fruitfulness.

### *It Is the Motivation Behind God's Discipline*

Owners of vineyards are continually pruning their vines of "sucker shoots"—leaves that grow off the vine but do not flower into fruit. They take up energy from the vine that could be directed toward producing fruit, so they are removed. The purpose of the vineyard is to grow grapes, not leaves. Then, at the end of the harvest, the pruning of the vines is done. Branches that bore fruit are cut off the vine so that new branches—larger and more fruitful—can grow the following year. And Jesus says that the Father is the vinedresser who continually prunes the branches (us) on the vine (Jesus) so we will bear more fruit.

Many Christians are distracted by "good" things in life that take energy away from producing fruit. When I first began in ministry, I didn't know how to say "No." I assumed anything anybody asked me to do for the Lord was something I was supposed to do.

I quickly learned that these "sucker shoots" could keep me from being fruitful in what God had called me to do. I also learned that God was very good at "pruning" my life of distractions—to bring my attention back to His primary calling for my life.

Sometimes fruitful Christians go through times of difficulty, of pruning, and they don't really understand why. It may be to prepare them to bear even more fruit. Some fruitless Christians never seem to have any difficulty. The reason is that no vinedresser is going to spend time pruning a vine that doesn't bear fruit (verse 2).

### It Is the Method of Touching Other People

We bear fruit as a result of the blessing of God. But our fruit is for the benefit of others, not only for ourselves. There is a tendency in the modern church to be focused on what God can do for me. But that is missing the point of bearing fruit. Vines and branches don't consume their own fruit—they bear fruit to be a blessing for others.

### It Is the Manifestation of Christ to the World

Once when typing a manuscript on my computer, the spell-checker changed all my uses of "fruit-bearing" to "fruit-eating"! That's an example of what too many Christians do who bear fruit for their own blessing. They become fruit eaters instead of fruit bearers. Jesus (the vine) imparts His life into us (the branches) for the purpose of manifesting His life to the world. If we fail to carry His life to others, we have failed to become fruit-bearers. When people in this world see us or are around us, they should be seeing the fruit of our being connected to Jesus Christ. That is the whole point of bearing fruit as a Christian.

### It Is the Means of Glorifying the Father

In verse 8 Jesus said that God is glorified when we bear much fruit. When we are doing what God has called us to do and spreading God's fruit around to be a blessing to others, then God gets the glory. Jesus brought glory to the Father by finishing the work He was given to do (John 17:4), and we can do the same thing. When we follow Jesus' example of fruit-bearing, we likewise bring glory to the Father.

# THE ILLUSTRATIONS OF FRUIT-BEARING IN THE BIBLE

I grew up in a Christian setting where fruitbearing was only interpreted one way: soul winning. You were bearing fruit for Christ if you were winning souls for Christ. But there are more ways than one to bear fruit. For example, Paul mentions nine different ways to manifest the fruit of the Spirit in our life in Galatians 5:22–23.

Following are five categories of the Christian life in which we ought to be able to see fruit being borne if we are genuine followers of Christ.

## Character

The kind of person I am gives strong indication as to whether Jesus Christ is indwelling my life. Every Christian ought to be able to give testimony of the changes in their life since coming to know Christ. The fruit of the Spirit do not come naturally in our life. In fact, Paul contrasts the fruit of the Spirit with the "fruit" (works) of the flesh in Galatians 5. If anyone is still manifesting the works of the flesh after years of professing to be a Christian, there should be cause for concern.

## Conduct

Paul prays a wonderful prayer in Colossians 1:10: "That you may walk worthy of the Lord, fully pleasing Him, being fruitful in every good work and increasing in the knowledge of God." We learn in Ephesians 2:8–10 that we are saved *by* grace, *through* faith, *for* good works. While we are not saved by our works, our lives are definitely supposed to manifest the works God has saved us to perform. Our conduct should be a reflection of our union with Christ who is living His life through us (Galatians 2:20).

## Contributions

Lest you think I am forcing the idea of fruit to include financial giving, I turn your attention to Philippians 4:15–17. Paul, while languishing in prison, was ministered to by the church at Philippi with gifts for his support. And Paul, in thanking them, wrote, "Not that I seek the gift, but I seek the fruit that abounds to your account" (verse 17). Paul was grateful for their gifts but even more grateful that the fruit they shared with him would abound to their account in heaven, that they would receive credit for blessing Paul with the fruit with which they had been blessed by God.

Generosity with time, talent, and treasure is an indication of our recognition that all we have comes from God and is to be used as a blessing for others. Because it is so hard for us to release our finances, the sharing of our money is perhaps a very significant indicator of God's work in our lives. Holding tightly to what we have is not God's way, it is man's way. As long as we are being a channel for sharing financial fruit with others, God will never let the supply run dry.

## Communication

Did you know the Bible calls what comes out of our mouth "the fruit of our lips"? (Hebrews 13:15). Specifically, in that context, it is referring to praise that we offer to God. In the Old Testament, when the saints came to worship God, they brought the fruit of their flocks and their fields as sacrifices to God. In the New Testament, we bring the fruit of our lips as a sacrifice of praise and worship. When we sing the praises of God and declare His greatness through preaching, we are offering the fruit of our lips as a sacrifice to Him.

To attend the gathering of the church of Jesus Christ on Sunday and not join in the praise that is being offered is reason for concern. Every true believer should be eager to offer praise to the God who has done so much for him.

## Converts

Last, but certainly not least, we note the category of fruitbearing that is most commonly thought of: winning souls for Christ. Paul wrote to the Romans, having never visited Rome before, that he hoped to visit them and "have some fruit among [them]" (Romans 1:13). He was referring to spreading the Gospel farther and winning more converts among the population of Rome.

Nothing makes Christians more fearful today than the thought of sharing their faith with a nonbeliever. It was something I had to learn to do after four years of Bible college and four years of seminary. I used Dr. James Kennedy's *Evangelism Explosion* material and committed it to memory so I would know what to say when sharing my faith. I knew witnessing for Christ was something God wanted me to do, and I just asked Him to help me—and He did. The first church I pastored grew primarily as a result of winning new believers to Christ through the efforts of many who went out into the community on a regular basis to share their faith.

An interesting thing about fruit is that it has within it the seeds that will create more fruit. So when we win someone to Christ we are planting seeds that bear even more fruit in succeeding spiritual generations. But the Gospel is just one generation away from stopping its advance into the kingdom of darkness around the world. What if every Christian alive today never shared the Gospel again? On the other hand, what if every Christian alive today shared the

Gospel with one person every day for the rest of their lives? Think how much spiritual fruit would be borne!

After reviewing this list of five ways that fruit-bearing should be evident in your life—character, conduct, contributions, communication, and converts—you should have some sense of whether or not you are a genuine Christian. Remember what Jesus said: You will know them by their fruits. Apple trees produce apples, orange trees produce oranges, and "Christian trees" produce the fruit of Jesus Christ in their life. If none of these evidences are present in your life, there should be serious concern about your spiritual state of being.

This message is not to put you under a yoke of guilt. Rather, it is to encourage you to do what the apostle wrote to the Corinthians: "Examine yourselves as to whether you are in the faith" (2 Corinthians 13: 5). If you and I are true branches of the vine that is Jesus Christ, then His life will flow through us and out to the world.

1. Read John 15:1–7.

   a. Who is the owner of the vineyard? (verse 1)

   b. What prerogative does He have as He finds branches that are not bearing fruit? (verse 2a)

   c. How do you interpret this action on God's part? How would you relate it to Isaiah 5:1–7?

   d. What does God do to the branches that are bearing fruit? (verse 2b)

   e. Count the number of times the word "abide" is used in these verses. How would you define what it means to abide in Christ?

f.  What promise is made to those who abide in Christ, the vine? (verse 7b)

g.  What condition is placed on receiving the benefits of that promise? (verse 7a)

h.  How does abiding in Christ shape the kinds of things we would ask God for in prayer?

i.  How would you define the meaning of "My words abide in you?" Is this how disciples of Jesus are identified in the world?

2.  Read Matthew 7:15–20.

    a.  What is the context of this passage? (verse 15)

b. Explain the principle from nature that Jesus uses to help identify false prophets. (verses 16–17)

c. What should you assume about the spiritual integrity of someone who manifests carnal fruit in his life?

d. How does the apostle James make this same point using different metaphors and context? (James 3:8–12)

3. Read Matthew 12:33–37.

a. What contradiction did Jesus point out in the lives of the Pharisees? (verse 34a, 35)

b. What did Jesus identify as the source of all fruit, be it good or bad? (verses 34b–35)

c. What parallel do you find between verse 33 and Revelation 3:16? What does God seem to judge more strongly than outright unbelief?

4. Read Matthew 13:1–23.

a. How does Jesus define the levels of fruitfulness in this parable? (verses 8, 23)

b. What conditions can cause no fruit to be borne? (verses 19, 21, 22)

c. What seems to be the determining factor in the amount of fruit that is brought forth? (verses 8, 23)

d. Compare the soil in this parable with Jesus' reference to the heart in Matthew 12:34–35. Are they the same?

e. How do you keep the soil of your heart in such a condition that it will bring forth much fruit?

---

**DID YOU KNOW?**

Grape vines and vineyards played a significant role in ancient cultures. When the twelve Hebrew spies went up into the land of Canaan to spy out the land, they returned with a single cluster of grapes so large it had to be carried on a pole stretched between the shoulders of two of them! (Numbers 13:23) Israel was often referred to as God's vineyard that He planted for His own glory. He did everything necessary to produce good fruit in His vineyard, but it yielded only fruit that was bad. Therefore He allowed it to be overrun and destroyed (Isaiah 5). Jesus picked up on this image of the vineyard in His messages to Israel's leaders, alluding to himself as the Son of the vineyard owner (Mark 12).

# WORN-OUT KNEES— LIVING A YIELDED LIFE

### *John 14:12–14*

---

*In this lesson we discover why we are able to do greater works than Jesus did.*

---

## OUTLINE

Some might think it arrogant when they hear a Christian talk about doing greater works than Jesus. But it was Jesus himself who said His followers would do such works—not greater physical miracles, but spiritual miracles that would have their basis in a life of prayer.

I. **The Expectation of Greater Works**

II. **The Explanation of Greater Works**

III. **The Expression of Greater Works**
   A. The Reach of Our Ministry Is Greater
   B. The Result of Our Ministry Is Greater

IV. **The Execution of Greater Works**
   A. The Picture of Jesus on Earth
   B. The Picture of Jesus Back in Heaven

The city of Leipzig, Germany, had been the scene of a violent protest against Communist rule in 1953. But the protest was crushed by force. In four decades of fighting against Communist rule in East Germany, nothing changed behind the Iron Curtain. But in 1989, something happened that turned it in another direction. A group of Christians began meeting in a church where Johann Sebastian Bach used to play the organ. They began to hold candlelight prayer marches. The marches began very small but then grew: 10,000 marchers, then 30,000, then 50,000, then a half-million in Leipzig, and a million more in Berlin. And finally, in November, 1989, the Berlin wall itself, the reviled symbol of the Iron Curtain, yielded to a different kind of power and came crashing down in a million pieces.[1]

What force and violence could not do, praying people were able to accomplish. It was the power of worn-out knees, well documented in Scripture. The power of worn-out knees opened the Red Sea, brought water from the rock, and made the sun stand still. The power of worn-out knees brought fire from the sky for Elijah's sacrifice. It overthrew armies and healed the sick. The power of worn-out knees raised the dead and paved the way for the conversion of millions of Christians.[2] There is no power like the power of worn-out knees!

Prayer was at the heart of Jesus' final words to His disciples before His death. It is the central portion of his words, John 14:12–14, that forms the basis for this lesson on prayer. Jesus had told His disciples He was about to depart from them (John 13:33), that He was going to prepare a place for them where they would join Him (John 14:1–3).

When Philip realized that Jesus was leaving, he asked Jesus a question that led to the verses we'll study in this lesson. Philip said, "Lord, show us the Father, and it is sufficient for us" (John 14:8). Jesus' answer is the key to successful Christian ministry: "He who has seen Me has seen the Father" (verse 9). Philip didn't realize that he had been observing the work of the Father by observing the work of Jesus. Everything Jesus had done was the work of the Father.

Jesus' point to Philip was this: "I am not the source of My own sufficiency. Everything I did was the Father's initiative in Me." Jesus expressed this truth over and over during His ministry: He never acted on His own initiative, but only did that which the Father was doing (John 5:19, 30; 8:28; 12:49).

The key to Jesus' power on earth was His relationship to the Father in heaven. So Jesus was saying to Philip, "It doesn't matter if I leave physically because it was never about Me. The Spirit whom the Father is sending will continue the work of the Father through you. You will do even greater works than I have done as the Father continues His work."

If Jesus hadn't made this last statement himself (verse 12), it would almost sound blasphemous—the idea that Jesus' followers would do greater works than He did. He was countering the idea that the disciples' greatest days of ministry had been in the past with Him. In fact, they were yet to come.

## THE EXPECTATION OF GREATER WORKS (JOHN 14:12a)

The expectation of "greater works" has caused no small amount of confusion and controversy in the body of Christ. After all, Jesus' works were unprecedented in their miraculous nature. Are we to expect the ability to do works greater than Jesus did? Some have suggested that we will do these "greater works" only if we have enough faith. But Jesus didn't say anything about having "great faith" or "enough faith." He said those who believe in Him would do these greater works. If faith were the issue, we would have to have greater faith than Jesus—not likely to be the case. He is making a simple statement: Those who believe in Me will do greater works than I have done.

Can we change water into wine? Raise the dead? Multiply loaves of bread and fish? Walk on a stormy sea? As great as Jesus' works were, they were all temporary. Think of Lazarus—the poor man was raised from the dead only to have to die again later! So the miracles were as much for a sign to those watching as they were for the recipients themselves. And Jesus said what we would do would result in an even greater impact than what He had done.

## THE EXPLANATION OF GREATER WORKS (JOHN 14:12b)

Jesus tied the "greater works" to His return to heaven: "because I go to My Father" (verse 12b). And the coming of the Spirit was dependent on His return to the Father. The Spirit had not yet come because Jesus had not yet returned to the Father (John 7:39; 16:7). When all was complete—Jesus' returning to the Father and the Spirit's coming from the Father—the followers of Jesus would be able to ask of Jesus His help in carrying out His will, continuing to do His works—even greater works than He did (verse 13).

# THE EXPRESSION OF GREATER WORKS (JOHN 14:12b)

Approximately forty days after Jesus told the disciples about the "greater works," He returned to heaven (Acts 1:3, 9). Then ten days later, on Pentecost, the Holy Spirit was poured out on the disciples (Acts 2), resulting in Peter's sermon—and 3,000 people were converted to Christ! Never in Jesus' ministry did 3,000 people believe in Him in a single day. The greater works had begun.

Here are two ways in which the followers of Jesus are doing greater works today than He did in His day.

## The Reach of Our Ministry Is Greater

Jesus' entire ministry was confined to a very small geographic area—Israel, or what we refer to as the Holy Land. But, as Martin Luther said, our ministry is in a much larger venue: "For Christ took but a little corner for himself to preach and to work miracles, and but a little time; whereas the apostles and their followers have spread themselves through the whole world."[3]

In less than 300 years, the ministry entrusted to eleven men had spread throughout the Roman Empire. Heathen temples were closed and converts numbered in the millions. The emperor Constantine made Christianity the official religion of Rome in the fourth century. Jesus' work was now being multiplied through the lives of millions of followers instead of being localized in himself. The reference to the church as the "body of Christ" is beautifully illustrated through the spread of the Gospel.

When I preach a message on Sunday in California, it is heard by several thousand people. But via radio, television, the Internet, and print ministries, that message is eventually received by hundreds of thousands more. Jesus knew that kind of multiplication would happen after He departed. He saw how the Holy Spirit would enlarge the ministry of His followers.

## The Result of Our Ministry Is Greater

Not only is the reach of our ministry greater but the result is as well. It was truly miraculous for Jesus to give sight to blind eyes, to cleanse a leper, to give hearing and speech to the deaf and mute, and to raise the dead. But it is an even greater miracle to see a person blinded by sin see and understand the gospel; to cleanse the heart from sin; to see sinners hear the gospel and then proclaim it to others; to see the spiritually dead raised to new life in Christ. The spiritual works we do are greater than the physical works Jesus did.

Today we take for granted the spiritual miracles that are done in our lives; we are more fascinated by the possibility of physical healings. But which will matter the most a million years from now? Would you rather live this life with a healed body or live forever with a healed soul? The miracle of spiritual regeneration is the greatest miracle in the world, and we get to participate in it.

# THE EXECUTION OF GREATER WORKS (JOHN 14:13–14)

The way we execute these "greater works" is through prayer: "Whatever you ask in My name, that I will do, that the Father may be glorified in the Son. If you ask anything in My name, I will do it" (John 14:13–14).

Just as Jesus had the opportunity to do the Father's work when He was on earth, so we now have the opportunity to do Jesus' work through the power of the Holy Spirit while we are on earth. In the Old Testament, the Holy Spirit did not permanently indwell believers. But in the New Testament, that would change. In John 14:17, Jesus told the disciples, "The Spirit of truth . . . dwells with you and will be in you." The Spirit dwelt with the disciples at the time Jesus was teaching them (prior to Pentecost), but He would be in them after Jesus returned to the Father and the Spirit came.

So it is the indwelling Spirit who makes the difference in our lives. It is better to have Jesus within us through the Spirit than beside us. And with Him living in us, we can do the "greater works" as we call on Him in prayer.

There are two images that will help us grasp the privilege we have.

## The Picture of Jesus on Earth

It helps to understand the flow of power for ministry when Jesus was on earth.

1. The Will of the Father

   The will of the Father was preeminent in Jesus' life. He never created His own ministry; He just did what the Father wanted Him to do (John 8:29; Hebrews 10:7).

2. The Power of the Holy Spirit

It was the Holy Spirit who empowered Jesus to do the Father's will (Luke 4:14). Yes, Jesus was God. But He had set aside the prerogatives of deity when He came to earth (Philippians 2:5–7) and depended on the Holy Spirit in His humanity. In order to ultimately identify with us as High Priest, He lived just as we live—in dependence upon the Spirit for power and obedience to do the will of God.

3. The Link of Prayer

Prayer was the link between the Father's will and the Son's work as seen so clearly in Jesus' prayer in the Garden of Gethsemane: "Nevertheless not My will, but Yours, be done" (Luke 22:42). Jesus counted on prayer as the source of strength that equipped Him to fulfill a partnership with God. He freely admitted His dependence. He said, "The Son can do nothing of himself, but what He sees the Father do" (John 5:19).

You say, "How did Jesus operate while He was on this earth?" The same way we're supposed to operate today. He sought the Father's will, He did the Father's work, He was filled with the Father's Spirit, and He prayed about it all.

## *The Picture of Jesus Back in Heaven*

That was Jesus on earth before He returned to heaven. But now that He is there, how is the accomplishment of His ministry different for those of us here on earth?

1. Jesus Wants to Do His Work Through Us

First of all, Jesus wants to do His work through us. That was His message to the disciples (and ultimately to us) in John 14. In fact, He wants to do more through us than He himself did.

2. The Father Has Sent His Spirit to Empower Us

The Spirit of truth changed His mode of operation after Pentecost. Rather than dwelling with believers as in the Old Testament, since Pentecost He has lived in believers. It is His power that allows us to do the works of Jesus in His absence.

3. Prayer Is the Link Between the Father's Will and Our Work

Jesus said in John 14:13, "And whatever you ask in My name, that I will do, that the Father may be glorified in the Son." Jesus is at the right hand of the Father in heaven but comes to live in us through the person of His Spirit. So we have this powerful link to the will of the Father. Just as Jesus knew what the Father's will was for Him (what works He should do), so we can know as well. And the way we know is through prayer.

Jesus promised that whatever we ask in His name, He will do. That doesn't mean every capricious, self-centered request we want. It means the things we want to know about doing His will, about doing His works as His followers on earth in His absence. And when we pray and ascertain the will and works of God that we should be doing, the Holy Spirit helps us to accomplish those works by His power.

If we want our life to count while we're on earth, then we have to stay connected to the Father, in Jesus' name, through the power of the Spirit. It's the way Jesus was able to know God's will, and it's the way we will know it as well. Just as the disciples had a head start on knowing the will of God by virtue of spending time with Jesus, so we can get "in the ballpark" regarding the will of God by studying His Word. Then, when we ask God for His help in accomplishing His will, the Holy Spirit is there to aid us.

Last, but not least, Hebrews 7:25 says that Jesus "always lives to make intercession" for us. That's how serious Jesus is about our accomplishing the "greater works" that He left for us to do. All that remains is for us to do them.

Notes:

1. Philip Yancey, *Prayer: Does It Make a Difference?* (Grand Rapids: Zondervan, 2006), 120.

2. David Jeremiah, *Prayer—The Great Adventure* (Sisters: Multnomah Publishers, 1997), 69.

3. John Marshall Lang, *The Last Supper of Our Lord: And His Words of Consolation to the Disciples* (New York: Macmillan, 1881), 157.

## APPLICATION

1. From the following verses in the gospel of John, note the various things Jesus said about His works:

   a. Verse 4:34. In what sense did Jesus use the word "food" to describe His life's goal? (See preceding context.)

   b. Verse 5:19. Jesus could obviously do things by himself. What did He mean by the use of "nothing"? Also, what did Jesus see the Father doing (miracles of healing, etc.?) What did He mean by this?

   c. Verse 5:30. What was Jesus' chief ambition in life?

   d. Verse 8:28. How do you think the Father taught Jesus what to speak? To what degree can He teach us as well?

   e. Verse 8:42. What sense of destiny did Jesus have about His presence on earth?

   f. Verses 12:49–50. How confident was Jesus about the words He spoke? What would that kind of confidence add to the success of your relationships?

g. Verse 14:10. How could obeying the Father's will and doing His work lead to conflict in the world? How did they lead to conflict in His life? Which is more important—avoiding conflict or doing God's will?

h. Verse 16:13. In what way did Jesus describe the Spirit's role of ministry, making it parallel to His own?

i. How does the word "submissive" describe Jesus and the Holy Spirit's attitude in their ministries?

j. What does Hebrews 5:8 add to your understanding of the humanity of Jesus' submission?

k. In what way was Jesus' humanity different from ours? (Luke 1:35)

l. Which of the following statements do you think best describes Jesus' humanity—and why?

- Jesus was not able to sin.

- Jesus was able not to sin.

m. Which of the statements best describes the Christian who is submissive to the Father's will?


2. Read Romans 8:26–27.

   a. What does the word "weaknesses" suggest about our knowledge of knowing God's will in a fallen world?


   b. How does the Spirit aid us in those moments? (verse 26)


   c. Why is it invaluable to have the Spirit interceding for us (in terms of God's will)? (verse 27)


3. What good news about the Spirit's ministry is found in John 3:34?


---

### DID YOU KNOW?

When Jesus said His followers would do "greater" works than His, He used a form of the Greek adjective *megas*, from which we get the popular English suffix "mega." *The American Heritage Dictionary* says "mega" means "surpassing other examples of its kind." So, we have churches and mega-churches; musical hits and mega-hits; normal houses and mega-houses. There is even a Mega Society of twenty-six members with I.Q.'s in the one-in-a-million range. So when Jesus said we would do greater works than His, they were to be mega-works: greater in reach and result than the works He himself did.

# WORN-OUT KNEES— LIVING A PEACEFUL LIFE

*Philippians 4:6–9*

*In this lesson we discover
how to experience the peace of God.*

## OUTLINE

Most of the world's discussion about peace these days centers around the absence of wars between nations. But the Bible focuses on a different kind of peace—a personal peace that is not dependent on what is happening in the world around us: the peace of God from the God of peace.

I. **The Problem: Worry**

II. **The Prescription: Prayer**
   A. Prayer
   B. Supplication
   C. Requests
   D. Thanksgiving

III. **The Program: Right Thinking and Right Action**
   A. To Avoid Anxiety, We Must Think Proper Thoughts
   B. To Avoid Anxiety, We Must Do Proper Things

IV. **The Promise: Peace**
   A. God's Protection
   B. God's Presence
   C. God's Peace

Tom Landry, the first coach of the Dallas Cowboys professional football team, is one of my all-time sports heroes. You can see why I admire him from this statement of his:

"Most of the athletes who fail to become winners are those athletes whose fears and anxieties prevent them from reaching their potential. I overcame my fears and my anxieties by a commitment to something far greater than winning a football game. I overcame them by my commitment to Jesus Christ." [1]

Tom Landry is right! The answer to fear and anxiety is a commitment to Jesus Christ, yet many Christians still wrestle with fear and anxiety. And it must not be just modern Christians since Paul wrote to the Philippians about this very subject—the text we'll be looking at in this lesson.

The Philippians had reasons to be tempted toward anxiety. Philippi was a Roman colony in the days of emperor Nero, whose persecutions were being felt all over the Empire. Christians never knew when Nero's cauldron of hatred might boil over. They needed to know how to trust God with every possible point of stress in their lives, and so do we.

## THE PROBLEM: WORRY

Paul gets right to the point: "Be anxious for nothing" (verse 6). "Anxious" is a synonym for "worry"; so Paul is saying, "Don't worry about anything." Paul might have been thinking of the words Jesus spoke to Martha: "Martha, Martha, you are worried and troubled about many things" (Luke 10:41).

I've seen research studies through the years that suggest that forty percent of the things people worry about never happen. Thirty percent are beyond one's control. Twelve percent have to do with anxiety about health issues even though the person is fine. Ten percent is unfounded worry about friends or relatives. That leaves eight percent of the things people worry about actually having a foundation in reality—which means ninety-two percent have no basis in reality and never happen!

Worry takes tomorrow's troubles and makes them today's experience in a very destructive way. All of us have moments of immediate concern and worry. But what we have to address is succumbing to worry—allowing it to become all-consuming in our life.

# THE PRESCRIPTION: PRAYER

Just as the problem is simple, so is the prescription: prayer. Don't worry about anything, Paul says, but pray about everything. These two great contrasts spell out Paul's strategy for a successful Christian life. Everything is included in prayer so that everything can be excluded from care!

An issue of *Newsweek* some time ago devoted its cover story to prayer. It included these words from a research study that was conducted on prayer: "In allegedly rootless, materialistic, self-centered America, there is also a hunger for a personal experience of God that prayer seeks to satisfy . . . . Serious prayer usually begins after the age of thirty when the illusion that we are masters of our own fate [disappears] and adults develop a deeper need to call on the Master of the Universe. In an age of relativism, God remains for many the one true absolute. And in an era of transience and divorce, God can be the only place left to turn for unconditional love."

Paul uses four different words to describe the kind of prayer that keeps worry at bay.

## Prayer

"Prayer" is the most general word used to describe reverent words addressed to God. It speaks to the frame of mind of the one praying—coming to God with reverence and respect. In our casual day and age, we've lost a bit of that aspect of approaching God. But Paul's words remind us of the need for reverence.

## Supplication

"Supplication" means to entreat—to come before someone who has everything and request the things that you need, the picture of a servant approaching a master with a request. The verb form of the word means to want, so a supplication is a request.

## Requests

And here Paul refers specifically to the requests we bring before God. We sometimes forget to pray specifically. I'm not sure why we do that with God when we don't do it in any other area of life. We don't ask our spouse, "Honey, would you pick up some groceries on the way home?" We say, "Would you pick up some bread and apples and milk and coffee." When we are tempted to worry, we need to tell God specifically, why—and ask for His help with that specific concern. Journaling—writing out my prayers on a daily basis—has helped me to go slowly and formulate my prayers in a specific manner.

### Thanksgiving

"Thanksgiving" is the most important of the four words. I have circled the little word "with" in verse 6 in my Bible because it is so important—"with" thanksgiving. Thanksgiving is the attitude that permeates all kinds of communication with God: prayer, supplication, requests, or any other. It is the attitude of gratitude that shows we are conscious of how God has blessed us. In times of worry or anxiety, it's easy to forget how blessed we really are. Staying in a mindset of thanksgiving puts our worries in proper perspective.

The worst thing that could happen to a Christian in this life is that we could die and go to heaven to be with Jesus. In light of that staggering truth, what worry is there that deserves the investment of our mental and emotional energy? What God has already provided for us is far beyond anything that might befall us in this life. Having the promise of eternal life is a far greater blessing than any potential calamity in the future.

## THE PROGRAM: RIGHT THINKING AND RIGHT ACTION

To work out Paul's prescription for prayer requires two things: thinking the right thoughts and doing the right things.

### To Avoid Anxiety, We Must Think Proper Thoughts

The word "meditate" in verse 8 is a word that means to carefully ponder, consider, and give proper weight and value to. Paul lists six categories of ideas and concepts that the Christian should meditate on as a defense against worry and anxiety.

1. Whatever Things Are True

   True things are reality, not fantasy or that which is unknown. When we worry about unknowns in the future, we are not worrying about truth. Reality is what is true today—like God and His promises.

2. Whatever Things Are Noble

   Noble things are honorable things. We've lost a lot of ideas like nobility and honor in our modern societies. If we are thinking on higher things, not debased things of this world, our thoughts will be noble and honorable.

3. Whatever Things Are Just

   Just things are righteous things. We cannot meditate on unrighteousness and expect to live a life of spiritual peace and tranquility.

4. Whatever Things Are Pure

   As in the case of Philippi in Paul's day, living in our culture means being surrounded by impurity. Keeping our minds focused on pure thoughts is essential to a life of peace.

5. Whatever Things Are Lovely

   Lovely things are pleasing and orderly. This is the only time this word is used in the New Testament, and it is certainly reflective of how God's rule is orchestrated, how heaven must look.

6. Whatever Things Are of Good Report

   Things of good report come from words meaning "fair speaking" or "good thinking." Things like true and honest and fair conversation come to mind; things like gossip and untruths do not.

It is impossible to live a peaceful life if we are filling our minds with lies, base thoughts, unrighteousness, ugliness, impurity, gossip, and speculation. Without even trying, our minds can become filled with these kinds of thoughts by simply living in our world. So we have to do more than just ignore the bad thoughts. We have to go on the offensive and seek to fill our minds with positive thoughts— thoughts that meet the high standards on Paul's list.

The best way to do that, of course, is by meditating on and memorizing the Word of God. There are more ways to fill our minds with God's Word than ever before in history. We can read it in our personal Bible or on numerous sites on the Internet, listen to it on cassettes or CD's or portable digital audio player, take it in as part of biblically-based devotional material or music, and memorize it using flash cards. There is no excuse today for any Christian not to fill his or her mind with the purity of God's Word.

Are you familiar with "white noise"? It's a technological development used to cancel out high-volume sounds in certain settings. White noise is generated by machines at a certain frequency that literally cancels out the noise at the same frequency in the room. That's what the Word of God does in our mind—it cancels out the "noise" our mind collects from living in this world. Scripture lowers the volume on thoughts that compete for our mental and spiritual attention.

Pastor Kent Hughes has made a suggestion for reading verse 8 in a helpful way—by flipping the words from the positive to the negative: "Finally, brothers, whatever is untrue, whatever is ignoble, whatever is wrong, whatever is impure, whatever is unlovely, whatever is not admirable, if there is anything shoddy or unworthy of praise, do not think about these things." [2] In addition to knowing what we should think about, this rendering adds what we shouldn't think about.

We may not be able to control the thoughts that pop into our mind, but we can definitely control the thoughts we purposely introduce into our mind and continue to dwell on. Those choices are important because it is our thoughts that determine our actions.

### To Avoid Anxiety, We Must Do Proper Things

Paul gives us a list of the kinds of behaviors that will bolster our defenses against anxiety: the things the Philippians had learned, received, heard, and seen in the life of the apostle himself. Paul doesn't say to think about these things, he says to "do" them (verse 9). Praying about everything with thanksgiving, filling our mind with godly thoughts, and practicing godly behavior will keep us from falling into worry.

To discover what those behaviors are, we need to read the Word of God. Philippians itself is filled with them—things the Philippians had "heard" from Paul. And we hear them, too, by reading what Paul wrote to the churches in his letters. You will not find any anxiety-producing behavior when reading the Word of God.

# THE PROMISE: PEACE

There are three benefits that accrue to those who will commit themselves to godly praying, thinking, and living.

### God's Protection

In verse 7 Paul says that God's peace will "guard your hearts and minds through Christ Jesus." "Guard" is a military term that means to camp or to garrison. God's peace will be like a troop of soldiers camping around your heart and mind, keeping out the worrisome thoughts of the day. Picture the vigilance with which armed soldiers stand guard around their camp in times of war. It is that picture Paul is painting here—and God's peace is the soldier marching back and forth, protecting your heart and mind from worry and anxiety. And that peace is established after we have prayed about everything and committed our worries to God.

## God's Presence

In verse 9 Paul says "the God of peace will be with you" when we do the things he outlines in that verse—specifically, incorporating into our lives the behaviors and disciplines we have heard and seen in his godly lifestyle.

Note two things in verses 7 and 9: "the peace of God" (verse 7) and "the God of peace" (verse 9). If we have the God of peace, then by default we have the peace of God. And we can't have the peace of God without having the God of peace. So they become two sides of the same coin: the presence of God and all the benefits that come with it. When you pray, think, and behave in a godly fashion, God's presence will be in your life. I have seen this over and over in my life—watching godly people go through extremely difficult circumstances without resorting to worry and anxiety. Why are they able to do this? Because they know the God of peace and, as a result, have the peace of God guarding their heart and mind.

And the sense of God's presence seems deeper when we are in the midst of trials and difficulties. God himself is no more present at one time than He is at another. But our realization of, and dependence on, His presence certainly changes. It seems that pressures in life can drive us toward God in a way that causes us to experience His peace in deeper ways.

## God's Peace

Finally, besides the protection and presence of God's peace, there is the peace of God itself. The peace of God "surpasses all understanding," meaning it is inexplicable—impossible to explain. When someone says, "How did you get through that situation without losing your mind?" you have to say, "I can't really explain it. I just know God was with me and gave me His peace." The peace of God surpasses our understanding—a peace, Jesus said, that is unlike the world's "peace" (John 14:27).

So when the problem is worry, the prescription is prayer, the program is right thinking and right doing, and the promise is peace —the protection of God's peace, the presence of God's peace, and peace itself. You can be in life's most difficult situation and experience peace that only God can give if you have taken the prescription, worked the program, and believed the promise.

Notes:

1. Howard E. Ferguson, *The Edge* (Cleveland: Getting the Edge Co., 1983), 4:9.
2. R. Kent Hughes, *The Disciplines of a Godly Man* (Wheaton: Crossway, 1991), 72–73.

## APPLICATION

1. Read Romans 8:31–39.

   a. Why is verse 31 a good summary statement for why Christians should not worry?

   b. What is the evidence in verse 32 that God stands ready to meet every need we have?

   c. What kinds of needs are you tempted to worry about in either the present or the future?

   d. Which of those needs do you believe falls outside the bounds of the promise in verse 32?

   e. How much worry is generated by wondering how God will meet a need you have? Why is trust a key element in a life of peace?

   f. List the things Paul says will never separate us from the love of Christ. (verse 35)

   g. Now list the things that you sometimes allow to separate you from a worry-free life in Christ—things you would list if you had been writing verse 35.

h. In terms of alleviating worry, what does it mean for Christ to be making intercession for you? (verse 34)

i. What is the implied answer to the question in verse 35?

j. What is the difference between the list in verse 35 and the list in verses 38–39? Do you tend to worry more about "practical" matters or "theoretical" matters? How does God's love cover both?

2. What promise does Isaiah 26:3 make to those seeking peace?

a. What is man's part?

b. What is God's response?

c. "Perfect peace" in the Hebrew is shalom shalom (shalom = peace). What does this repetition suggest in light of verses like Song of Solomon 1:1 and Revelation 19:16?

3. Read 2 Corinthians 10:3–6.
a. Why do worry and anxiety seem like a war at times?

b. In what way can worry become a "stronghold" (a fortress) in your mind? Are there any worries that have assumed that role in your life? (verse 4)

c. Describe what it is like to "argue" with your worries—when your worries challenge your "knowledge of God." (verse 5)

d. Describe the "argument" between truth and falsehood that took place in Genesis 3:1–5. (verse 5a)

e. What is our responsibility when those arguments occur? (verse 5b)

---

## DID YOU KNOW?

In the *Authorized (King James) Version* of the Bible, Philippians 4:6 says to "be careful for nothing." That sounds reckless: "Don't be a careful person." But that is an Old English way of saying "don't be anxious." The original Greek word for "to worry," *merimnao*, meant "to take thought or care." It was made from two words, *merizo*, to divide, and *nous*, mind. So to worry meant to have a divided mind, a mind pulled in two directions at once, a mind divided between healthy and unhealthy thoughts, a mind that tries to rest but is filled with worry, a mind divided between living in the present and worrying about the future.

# ROLLED-UP SLEEVES— LIVING AN AUTHENTIC LIFE

## *John 13:1–17*

*In this lesson we see history's greatest example of humble service.*

---

### OUTLINE

It's easy in our hurry-up world to rush by those in our path who need help, who need what only God can offer. Jesus showed His disciples what it means to serve others with humility, to set pride aside, and to let love be the motivation for reaching out—loving others the way He loves us.

  I. **A Persuasive Initiative for Rolled-Up Sleeves**

 II. **Some Practical Insights About Rolled-Up Sleeves**
    A. Rolled-Up Sleeves Will Test Your Authenticity
    B. Rolled-Up Sleeves Will Teach You Humility

III. **A Powerful Illustration of Rolled-Up Sleeves**

IV. **Some Personal Instructions Concerning Rolled-Up Sleeves**
    A. Knowledge Produces Accountability
    B. Example Increases Responsibility
    C. Obedience Determines Authenticity

J ames McGuiggan is a writer from Northern Ireland whose books have challenged my life. He wrote a book called *Jesus, Hero of Thy Soul* in which he says, "Having seen Jesus, knowing how He has lived His life here, we can't settle for less than a genuine pursuit of His likeness. His very presence among us forbids us from being just 'nice' people who do 'nice' things . . . The bland leading the bland, both falling into a 'nice' rut." [1]

That statement is a wonderful introduction to the theme of this lesson: how we live our life in this world. For many people, the only human image or likeness of Jesus Christ may be you or me. Therefore, it matters how closely our lives manifest His.

John 13–17 constitutes the Upper Room Discourse, the last extended teachings and conversation Jesus had with His disciples before His crucifixion. His public ministry is over, and He is conveying things that were only for the ears of His disciples.

Part of Jesus' teaching in John 13:1–8 was acted out by Him in a drama of sorts—a live demonstration of what it means to roll up one's sleeves and serve others. That is the message we must take into the world if people are going to see Jesus when they see us.

# A Persuasive Initiative for Rolled-Up Sleeves

Love was at the center of Jesus' serving His disciples—at the center of everything He did. He "loved His own . . . to the end" (verse 1). If we are going to serve others, our motivation must be the same as His: love. "To the end" is a Greek expression that refers not to time but to extent. Jesus loved His disciples with the full extent of His love; He loved them to the uttermost; He loved them unconditionally.

Love is a central theme in the gospel of John. The majority of the uses of the word "love" in the New Testament come from the pen of the apostle John. And it is fitting that love introduces the Upper Room Discourse in John 13:1 and concludes it in John 17:26. Perhaps the most famous of Jesus' words on love are in the context of the "new commandment" He gave the disciples to "love one another" (John 13:34–35).

Loving one another is not easy—some have called it the hardest thing in life to do. There are plenty of fleshly reasons to turn away from people who make themselves unlovable by their behavior or attitudes. Regardless, we are called to roll up the sleeves of our heart and love them anyway with a Christ kind of love. In the Upper Room, Jesus washed the feet of Peter, who denied Him three times, and Judas, who betrayed Him. That is the model we are to follow.

When we ask, "How?" the answer is "as I have loved you" (John 13:34). The "love of God" that "has been poured out in our hearts by the Holy Spirit" is the source of our love for others (Romans 5:5). It is not we who love, but Christ who loves in and through us (Galatians 2:20).

There's a movie called *The Princess Bride* in which the fair maiden, Buttercup, has a servant named Wesley. Whenever she asks him to do anything for her, his reply is always the same: "As you wish; as you wish." One day she discovers that when Wesley says, "As you wish," what he really means is, "I love you." And that's the way it is with Jesus and His followers. When we say, "As you wish" out of obedience as servants of Christ, we are saying, "I love You, Lord." When we love Him, we are motivated to love others as He has loved us.

# SOME PRACTICAL INSIGHTS ABOUT ROLLED-UP SLEEVES

Service to others will accomplish good for the person(s) served, but it will accomplish two things in your life as well.

## *Rolled-Up Sleeves Will Test Your Authenticity*

In John 12:36, there is an interesting sentence: "These things Jesus spoke, and departed, and was hidden from them." The point is that Jesus left the public eye and went into seclusion with His disciples in the Upper Room. He didn't wash the disciples' feet on national television; He didn't hold a press conference to announce what He was doing. Serving His disciples outside the public's view was a testimony to the authenticity of the act.

There is nothing wrong with letting others see our good works (Matthew 5:16). The point is that we are not to do them for that reason (Matthew 6:1–8). We can get our reward from men or from God. If we seek to get our reward from men by doing our good works in their sight, there will be no reward from God. We can have our reward now or have it later, and the choice we make will reveal the authenticity of our service for God.

# Rolled-Up Sleeves Will Teach You Humility

The second thing that true service will do is teach us humility. John the apostle tells us that Jesus knew "the Father had given all things into His hands" and that He was "going to God" (John 13:3). Yet He was the one who stooped down to take on the role of a servant and wash His disciples' feet. His humility is contrasted plainly with the disciples' behavior during that last Passover meal: They were engaged in a "dispute" among themselves as to which of them was the greatest (Luke 22:24).

Can you imagine? The disciples were there to share a meal with the greatest person on earth who was about to wash their feet as an act of humble service—and they were arguing about who among them was the greatest!

The Bible tells us we are to be clothed with humility (Colossians 3:12). Someone has written, "If most believers of this generation were clothed in their own humility, they would be arrested for indecent exposure."

Samuel Logan Brengle was a Methodist minister who left a busy pastorate to join the Salvation Army in England in 1878. William Booth, the founder of the Salvation Army, almost wouldn't accept him into the corps saying, "You've been your own boss too long." To test Brengle's humility, Booth assigned him the task of polishing the other trainees' boots. Later, telling his own story, Brengle said he wondered, "Have I followed my own fancy across the Atlantic in order to black boots?" And then, as in a vision, he saw Jesus bending over the feet of rough unlettered fishermen, washing their feet. "Lord," he cried out in his heart, "You washed their feet: I'll black their boots." [2]

In the eyes of Jesus, the way down is the way up. True greatness only comes on the heels of true humility. I remember having thoughts akin to those of Brengle when I pastored my first church. The seven families that constituted our church met in two double-wide trailers. I arrived in the winter and discovered I was not only expected to be the pastor but the plumber as well. Lying under those trailers wrapping the water pipes so they wouldn't freeze and break, I remember thinking, "Lord, is this why I spent four years in seminary—to do this?" And His answer was a simple, "Yes— that and more."

All of us have to learn that humility is a prerequisite to true service. And, in due course, God gives all who follow Jesus the opportunity to learn that lesson.

# A POWERFUL ILLUSTRATION OF ROLLED-UP SLEEVES

In verses 4–5, we have the powerful illustration of Jesus' humble service: His rising from His seat, taking a towel and basin of water, washing the disciples' feet, and wiping them with a towel.

It was the custom in that day for dinner guests to recline on the floor around a low table, or a spread of vessels of food placed on the floor. So the disciples' feet would not have been under a table as they would be in a modern dining setting. Jesus took the basin of water and towel and began to go around the perimeter of where they were reclining, washing the feet of each in turn—the work of the lowest slave in a household.

The disciples understood the role Jesus was taking on, washing the dust of the streets off their feet. The One they called Master and Teacher and Lord was doing something they themselves had never, and probably would never, have done for each other.

After Jesus finished His humble task, He sat down among them and asked them a question—a question that leads us to some applications for our life from what He did: "Do you know what I have done to you?" (verse 12)

# SOME PERSONAL INSTRUCTIONS CONCERNING ROLLED-UP SLEEVES

There are three insights to be gleaned from Jesus' demonstration to His disciples, insights we must understand if we are to roll up our sleeves in this world as He did.

## Knowledge Produces Accountability

Verses 12 through14 teach us that our knowledge of something produces accountability. The word "ought" near the end of verse 14 is a key word in this point: "You also ought to wash one another's feet." The knowledge of who Jesus was and who they were, and the fact that He washed their feet in spite of the gulf that separated them, made them accountable to do the same for each other.

## Example Increases Responsibility

In verses 15–16, Jesus takes it a step farther: "For I have given you an example, that you should do as I have done to you. Most assuredly, I say to you, a servant is not greater than his master, nor is he who is sent greater than he who sent him." The disciples would never be able to say they didn't know how or what to do in terms of service. They had seen the ultimate example of humility before their very eyes and were therefore responsible to do the same.

## Obedience Determines Authenticity

The key to the issue of humble service is in verse 17: "If you know these things [the things I have taught you by washing your feet], blessed are you if you do them." Jesus didn't say, "Blessed are you if you think about them, marvel at them, talk about them after I'm gone, or tell your grandchildren about them." He said, "Blessed are you if you do them."

Blessedness in the Christian life comes from obedience. Authenticity comes from following the steps and commands of Jesus. How will the world get an authentic picture of Jesus if we, His followers, do not do the things He did—and told us to do? It's easy to get a vicarious blessing out of reading a story like this one, and there's nothing wrong with that. But if we stop there, we will miss the greater blessing that comes from doing what Jesus said to do.

Much of modern societies' energy is spent in the pursuit of happiness. But the longer I walk with the Lord, the more I realize that happiness isn't found in pursuing it. Happiness is a by-product, so to speak, of obedience to God. Blessedness (happiness) comes from God when we align ourselves with Him and His plan for our life—and part of that plan is being an ambassador for Jesus Christ (Ephesians 6:20), revealing His life to the world.

Part of revealing Christ to the world is the responsibility to be a servant, just as He was. And it is in serving others that happiness is found. What could provide a greater blessing than meeting the needs of others—especially those who have no way to make do for themselves or cannot repay your service. That's the way Jesus served and the way we are to serve as well.

The story of Jesus' washing the disciples' feet can get under our skin; indeed, it should get under our skin! There's something contrary to human nature about serving other people in such a humbling manner. But that's the whole point, isn't it? There's nothing in this world that would motivate us to serve in such a manner. But if we are going to follow Jesus, we are going to have to be pricked and challenged and made uncomfortable. We are going to have to deny ourselves, like Jesus did, and experience the discomfort that comes when Jesus does things through us that we would not normally do ourselves. But then we get to enjoy the blessing that follows.

Every Christian knows someone who needs a special touch from the Lord. You can probably think of someone right now in that category. Perhaps you passed someone this week with whom you didn't want to make eye contact because you knew they needed help—and you felt too busy or to awkward to stop and offer a helping hand or word. What we learn from Jesus' example with His disciples is that we have to stop and help. Jesus said, "Blessed are you if you do [acts of service like I have just demonstrated to you]."

There may be someone in your neighborhood or a coworker who is going through a difficult time. It's difficult to reach out to people we don't know all that well. But think of the number of people Jesus served and helped who were complete strangers. All it takes is for us to get past our fears and reach out in order to find ourselves representing Jesus to the world.

Take a look at your own sleeves today. Are they neatly starched and buttoned or are they rolled up, making your hands free to become the hands of Jesus to a hurting world?

Notes:

1. Jim McGuiggan, *Jesus, Hero of Thy Soul* (West Monroe: Howard Publishing, 1998), 4.

2. Quoted in R. Kent Hughes, *John: That You May Believe* (Wheaton: Crossway Books, 1999), 3–6.

## APPLICATION

1. What do 1 John 4:8 and 16 reveal about the very nature of God?

    a. Therefore, what was the motivation for everything Christ did while on earth?

    b. What does John 3:16 say about God's reason for sending Jesus to earth?

    c. What is the evidence that God lives in us? (1 John 4:12)

    d. By what act on Christians' parts will the world come to know that we are followers of Jesus? (John 13:35)

    e. What personal test can we apply to ourselves to confirm that we have new life from God? (1 John 3:14)

    f. What judgment is made about anyone who does not love others? (1 John 3:14; 4:20)

    g. Why is it easier to say, "I love God" than to say, "I love my brother"?

    h. Why did God make loving our brother a test for whether we love Him?

2. Read Deuteronomy 8:2–3.

   a. What was God's purpose in leading the children of Israel into the wilderness when they left Egypt? (verse 2b)

   b. What two spiritual means did God use to accomplish that purpose? (verse 2a)

   c. What practical form did those means take when they were in the wilderness? (verse 3a)

   d. What did God want Israel to learn through this humbling experience? (verse 3b)

   e. What was the first thing required of the people of God in the Old Testament in order to have God intervene on their behalf? (2 Chronicles 7:14)

   f. What do you learn about God's commitment to the humble from verses like Psalm 25:9; 147:6; 149:4; Proverbs 3:34?

   g. How does Matthew 18:4 stand in stark contrast to Luke 22:24?

   h. How is Jesus washing the disciples' feet an illustration of Matthew 18:4?

i. How is Luke 14:11 an illustration of "doing it the hard way or the easy way" when it comes to becoming humble? What would the easy way be?

3. What will the humble do according to Romans 12:16?

   a. How did Jesus demonstrate His own humility? (Philippians 2:8)

   b. Why is humility necessary even when correcting those who are in error? (2 Timothy 2:25)

4. How would you evaluate your own humility in light of Jesus' example in John 13?

---

### DID YOU KNOW?

The washing of the saints' feet has been practiced in a scattered fashion throughout church history. Besides the John 13 reference, the only other place it is mentioned in Scripture is 1 Timothy 5:10, there spoken of as a sign of piety in a widow. In post-apostolic Christianity, there are various references in the writings of church fathers to foot-washing, but not enough to consider it an established practice. Today, some Christian denominations practice foot-washing on Maundy Thursday, the day before Good Friday, in commemoration of the Last Supper. Others practice it regularly as part of the Communion service. Across Christendom, foot-washing is not recognized as a sacrament (like baptism or Communion), but as a memorial practice.

# ROLLED UP SLEEVES—
# LIVING A LIFE OF SERVICE

*Romans 12:6–7; 1 Corinthians 12:28; 1 Peter 4:11*

*In this lesson we discover what is at the heart
of Christian service.*

## OUTLINE

One of the hallmarks of modern societies is that most people are out
to succeed. But there's a rare category of individuals who are out to
help others succeed—those with the spiritual gift of helps. They
exemplify the principles that all servants of Christ should practice.

I. **Biblical Portraits of the Gift of Helps**
   A. In the Life of Onesiphorus
   B. In the Life of Timothy

II. **Biblical Principles for the Gift of Helps**
   A. Servants Desire to Bring Glory to God
   B. Servants Discover That the Way Up Is the Way Down
   C. Servants Develop Strength Through Weakness
   D. Servants Derive Their Joy From the Development of Others

I received a letter a few years ago from two ladies, sisters, who had visited our church on a Sunday morning. They were staying at a hotel in San Diego and had taken public transportation to El Cajon, outside San Diego, where our church is located. After the Sunday service, they spent some time in our bookstore and looking around the campus. When they were ready to leave and return to San Diego, they discovered they had missed the transportation they needed. They were stranded in an unfamiliar place without a way to return to their hotel—when a member of our church came along and offered to take them where they needed to go. Their note was a word of thanks for the kindness of the woman who graciously served them that day—thanks which we happily passed on.

I wouldn't be surprised if the dear lady who helped those visitors had the spiritual gift of helps, or service. People with that gift seem to find opportunities to serve and help others without trying. While we don't all have the spiritual gift of helps, we are all called to serve one another with joy and humility.

The gift of helps is mentioned specifically in Romans 12:7 (called "ministry"), 1 Corinthians 12:28 ("helps"), and 1 Peter 4:11 ("ministry"). Here is how author Peter Wagner describes the gift of helps: "The gift of helps is the special ability that God gives to some members of the body of Christ to invest the talents they have in the life and ministry of other members of the body, thus enabling the person helped to increase the effectiveness of his or her spiritual gifts."

A person with this gift looks for ways he or she can contribute in a way that makes other people's ministries even more effective. There is likely a large number of people in every church with this gift because there is much ministry to be supported and accomplished.

# BIBLICAL PORTRAITS OF THE GIFT OF HELPS

In the New Testament, we can find sketches of individuals manifesting every spiritual gift, including the gift of helps.

## In the Life of Onesiphorus

Onesiphorus is mentioned only twice in the New Testament: 2 Timothy 1:16 and 4:19. The description of his service to the apostle Paul makes it easy to see why he had the gift of helps (2 Timothy 1:16–18): "He often refreshed me, and was not ashamed of my chain . . . he sought me out very zealously and found me . . . and you know very well how many ways he ministered to me at Ephesus."

Onesiphorus was a blessing to Paul. He wasn't ashamed that Paul was a prisoner. Instead, he sought Paul out and refreshed him in a multitude of ways. There is no doubt Onesiphorus was like a breath of fresh air to Paul when he was in prison. It's amazing to be around a person like that—someone who by his very presence seems to lift your spirits and encourage you to keep on keeping on. They stand in stark contrast to those who bring a sense of pessimism and heaviness into the room. Onesiphorus was the former kind—a person who brought energy and encouragement to every meeting.

I know we have these people in the church I pastor, and they are probably in your church as well. You may be one of these blessed saints! In my church, people with this gift send me notes to tell me that they appreciate my ministry, to encourage me to keep preaching the Word of God, to thank me for exercising my gifts for the Lord. Those little gestures are a source of pure refreshment for me, just as Onesiphorus was to Paul.

### *In the Life of Timothy*

I believe Timothy also had this gift. His relationship with Paul in the New Testament is a deep and long one—a mentor (Paul) and his protégé. Paul thought of Timothy as his own son (2 Timothy 1:2). He and Paul were soul mates in the work of the Gospel of Christ. Timothy is mentioned twenty-four times in the letters Paul wrote; and five times, Timothy is associated with Paul in the writing of his letters.

In Philippians 2:20, Paul says that Timothy is the only "like-minded" person he has who can go to Philippi in his place. Paul was saying that if they had Timothy, they had Paul. Timothy could speak for Paul in his absence. Timothy was a young man after Paul's own heart. The commentator William Hendrickson wrote these words about Timothy, as if they were spoken by the apostle Paul:

"No one is better qualified and more favorably disposed. Already as a child he was an eager student of the sacred writings . . . (2 Timothy 3:15). As he grew up, he was highly recommended by those who knew him best (Acts 16:2). Upon his conversion to the Christian faith, he became my beloved and faithful child in the Lord (1 Corinthians 4:17); and a little later, my special deputy and fellow worker (Romans 16:21), always ready to go wherever I sent him or to be left behind

wherever I told him to remain (Romans 16:21) . . . And
do not forget either that from the very founding of your
church he has known you, and you have known him; not
only was he present when your church was established
(Acts 16:11–40; 1 Thessalonians 2:2), but subsequently
he has also visited you upon more than one occasion
(Acts 19:21–22; 20:3–4; 2 Corinthians 1:1)."[1]

I believe there are four aspects of Timothy's life that reveal his
gift of helps.

### 1. His Compassion for Others

Again in Philippians 2:20, Paul mentions Timothy's desire
to "sincerely care" for the Philippians. And we note again that
Timothy was the only one to whom Paul could entrust
that mission. Paul must have seen in Timothy the gift of
helps, or ministry. Timothy apparently manifested a concern
for the spiritual welfare of the Philippians that was plainly
evident to Paul.

A person with the gift of helps does not serve for recognition;
his only desire is to help and support others. Timothy was
that kind of person—helping because it was an internal,
God-given motivation.

### 2. His Consecration to the Lord

In Philippians 2:21, Paul drew a contrast between Timothy
and other workers: "For all seek their own, not the things
which are of Christ Jesus." Timothy, on the other hand,
sought the things of Christ, not his own desires. It is no
wonder that Timothy was "well spoken of by the brethren
who were at Lystra and Iconium" (Acts 16:2).

Anyone who is seeking to help others and is not out to
promote himself is going to be "well spoken of " by those
around him. They stand out because of this. They are
people who serve with an open hand—letting God put
in and take away according to His plans and purposes.

### 3. His Commitment to the Gospel

Timothy was so linked with Paul because of his shared
commitment to the Gospel of Christ: "But you know his
proven character, that as a son with his father he served with
me in the gospel" (Philippians 2:22). The best way Timothy
knew to serve others was by sharing with them the Gospel.

4. His Concern for Paul

Near the end of Paul's life when he was in the Roman prison, he wrote his last letter to Timothy (2 Timothy). Timothy was a pastor in Ephesus, and there was nothing he wouldn't have done for Paul. Paul knew that and asked Timothy to bring with him the "the cloak . . . and the books, especially the parchments" (4:13).

Timothy was not too busy or important to stop what he was doing and serve his mentor, Paul. Some pastors might have said, "Sorry, Paul—I'll get one of my assistants to take these things to Rome." But Timothy was not too big or proud— like Jesus washing the feet of His disciples—to do the work of a servant.

In verse 21, Paul went on to ask Timothy to "do your utmost to come before winter." Paul was alone in a Roman prison and longed for the presence of his young friend. He knew he could ask anything of Timothy—not lording it over him, but as a friend—and Timothy would respond. It's a wonderful blessing to have people in your life whom you know love you and will come to your aid when you call them—people with the gift, or at least the spirit of the gift, of helps.

# BIBLICAL PRINCIPLES FOR THE GIFT OF HELPS

There are principles embedded in the heart of those with the gift of helps, but they apply to all Christians since all are called to serve.

## *Servants Desire to Bring Glory to God*

A true servant is one who desires to bring glory to his master. In the case of Christian service, a servant-Christian desires to bring glory to God. That's why a servant will serve without credit or self-promotion—he understands his role and embraces it fully.

When John the Baptist announced the coming of Jesus, the Messiah, he said, "He must increase, but I must decrease" (John 3:30). John knew his role was to introduce Jesus—to draw attention to Him. That's what servants do: make others successful in their task or mission. How many people do you know today who have that kind of perspective on their life?

Do you remember what Jesus said about our good works? He didn't say to let people "see your good works and glorify you." He said, "that they may see your good works and glorify your Father in heaven" (Matthew 5:16). That's what servants of God do. Everything in their life is done to glorify God.

## Servants Discover That the Way Up Is the Way Down

Servanthood illustrates one of the many paradoxes in the kingdom of God: The way up is the way down; the way forward is the way backward.

What does this mean? Jesus illustrated it in Matthew 20:26–28 where He taught that whoever wants to be great must first become a servant. He pointed out that He himself did not come to be served, but to serve—and He did so by "[giving] His life a ransom for many." A person with a servant's heart isn't looking to fight his way to the top. He or she is happy to serve with no recognition. Indeed, they are usually more comfortable serving that way. People with the gift of helps would often much rather be behind the scenes instead of being thrust out in front of people, expected to lead the way.

See if you can identify with this: "You can tell if you are a real servant by the way you act when someone treats you like one." Many people react poorly when they are treated like a servant, but those with the gift or the heart of helps do not. The amazing thing about Jesus was that He volunteered to be a servant (Philippians 2:5–8). He didn't have to decide how to respond to being treated like a servant because He voluntarily assumed that position. That's a good way to prepare for being treated like a servant: Assume the position on your own so you are merely being treated like what you have willingly become.

## Servants Develop Strength Through Weakness

The apostle Paul wrote the classic statement on this principle in 2 Corinthians 12:10: "Therefore I take pleasure in infirmities, in reproaches, in needs, in persecutions, in distresses, for Christ's sake. For when I am weak, then I am strong." While that sounds like a contradiction—being strong when you are weak—it is not.

It is when we are at our very weakest—through sickness, persecution, distress, tribulations—that we are able to be at our strongest through the power of God. When our human strength and endurance fails, we are able to realize the strength of God in our life, something I learned in my own experience with cancer.

Though I was never so weak physically as during that time, I was never so aware of the power of God at the same time—in ways I had never experienced before being in a state of weakness.

People who have the gift or heart of a servant know the limitations of their own strength. Depending on God is nothing to be embarrassed about—it's the only way to accomplish those things they desire to do, things that are beyond their abilities. So they welcome weakness! If that sounds strange, it's because it's the language of the kingdom of God, not of this world.

## Servants Derive Their Joy From the Development of Others

Finally, servants take great joy in seeing others succeed. The apostle Paul expressed this often in his writings—the joy he felt at the spiritual progress that others were making.

In Philippians 4:1, he called the Christians at Philippi his "beloved and longed-for brethren, my joy and crown." If Paul was going to wear a crown, it would not be the result of his accomplishments but the spiritual success of the Philippians. And in 1 Thessalonians 2:19, he wrote something similar: "For what is our hope, or joy, or crown of rejoicing? Is it not even you . . . ?" If a crown is something a normal person would enjoy or exalt in, then for Paul, people were his crown. As a servant-apostle of Christ, he enjoyed nothing more than seeing new Christians grow to maturity in Jesus.

Whether we have the gift of helps or not, you and I are called to manifest these principles of service.

Notes:

1. William Hendricksen, *New Testament Commentary-Exposition of Philippians* (Grand Rapids: Baker, 1962), 34.

1. Read Philippians 2:1–11.

   a. What is Paul's overall exhortation to the Philippians in verses 1–4?

   b. In verse 2 he wants them to be of the same _____ .

   c. In verse 3 the goal is for them to . . . .

   d. Verse 4 would have them looking out for . . . .

   e. With that context in mind, how do verses 5–11 serve as an example or illustration of Paul's exhortations in verses 1–4?

   f. In order to be like Christ, what must we have? (verse 5) What does verse 5 mean?

   g. Although He was "in the form of God," what did Christ *not* do? (verse 6)

   h. What "form" did Christ take in His incarnation? (verse 7)

i. Who did Christ look like when He came to earth? (verse 7b–8a; Isaiah 53:2)

j. What two acts, consistent with being a servant, did Christ perform when He came to earth? (verse 8)

k. And what did God do in response to Christ's servant acts? (verse 9)

l. Name the categories of beings who will one day bow before the servant Jesus? (verse 10) Who is included in these categories?

m. To what rank or position has God the Father exalted Jesus the Son because of the Son's humble obedience? (verse 8, 11)

n. Since Paul used Christ as an example of servanthood, might we expect God to bless our servanthood as He did Christ's?

o. What is the most challenging aspect for you of what Jesus Christ did as pictured in verse 7?

2. Read Matthew 20:20–28.
   a. Who were the "sons of Zebedee"? (verse 20; Mark 10:35)

b. What did their mother ask of Jesus? (verse 21)


c. What was the reaction of the other ten disciples to James and John's request? (verse 24)


d. What was characteristic of the Gentile rulers of the day? (verse 25)


e. How would greatness be defined for His disciples? (verse 26)


f. What must those who desire to be "first" do first? (verse 27)


g. How was Jesus an example of what He was saying to the disciples?


h. In what area do you hope to excel in your life? How might you make yourself a servant in that area?

---

### DID YOU KNOW?

There are seven Greek words in the New Testament used to refer to servants or service, the two most common being *doulos* (usually translated as "bondservant" or "slave") and *diakonos* (from which we get "deacon," usually translated as "servant" or "minister"). *Doulos* occurs thirty-two times in Paul's epistles and *diakonos* twenty-one times. Paul occasionally referred to himself as a *diakonos* (2 Corinthians 6:4; 11:23; Ephesians 3:7). But he more often, and much more personally and intensely, referred to himself as a bondservant of Christ (Romans 1:1; 2 Corinthians 4:5; Philippians 1:1). A bondservant was one who, though a free man, voluntarily submitted to his master in service.

# OPEN HANDS—LIVING A GENEROUS LIFE

### *Romans 12:8–13*

*In this lesson we learn how to live an open-handed life, receiving from the Lord and giving for the Lord.*

---

### OUTLINE

America is said to be the most generous nation on earth. Some people give to gain a tax deduction. Others give out of a sense of obligation. But a better reason to give is to be a channel of God's blessings. When God gives to us, part of what He gives is to go to those in need.

  I. **Generosity**

 II. **Sincerity**

III. **Humility**

IV. **Sympathy**

 V. **Hospitality**

We live in an age of contrasts: Never have modern societies been so wealthy in the things that don't matter and so poor in the things that do. We have unprecedented levels of material prosperity and unprecedented levels of moral and spiritual poverty. Some people, even some Christians, believe "that's just the way it is—that's life in the modern world."

But I believe God would show us a better way through the study of His Word. As Christians we are called to, "Go into all the world and preach the gospel to every creature" (Mark 16:15). That's the Great Commission. And in going we are to obey the two-part Great Commandment: loving God with all our heart, soul, and mind, and loving our neighbors as ourselves (Matthew 22:37–40). These two commandments reflect the organization of the Ten Commandments— the first four having to do with loving God, and the last six having to do with loving others (Exodus 20:1–17).

The definition of "loving your neighbor" has gone through various stages of discussion over the years. When I was growing up as a young Christian, something called the "social gospel" was being promoted. The idea was that serving people on a humanitarian basis (providing food, clothing, shelter, and other services) was the same as preaching the Gospel of salvation. Conservative, evangelical, Bible-believing churches and denominations did not support that movement, keeping the focus of the Gospel on sin and salvation.

Two things are important: We are never to lose sight of the biblical Gospel of salvation by grace through faith. But we are also supposed to love our neighbors—to meet whatever physical needs we can. We are asked to open our hands and our pocketbooks to provide for them as generously as possible. Jesus did both, giving prominence to the needs of man's spiritual life; but He did both. As James Stalker has written, "[Christ] would not allow [the] neglect of man to be covered by zeal for God, but [He] ever taught that the one who loves God must love his brother also." [1]

It may be that loving our brothers with a generous hand is the most challenging of the signs of life we are studying. We'll go, we'll pray, we'll serve—but giving up our "hard-earned" money? Now we're starting to get personal!

Think about an open hand: If I keep my hands open before God, He is free to take from my hands anything He wants. But, if my hand is open, God is also free to deposit into my hand anything, anytime, He wants. An open hand becomes a reservoir before God. He is continually placing resources in my hand and taking resources out for the benefit of others. But if I should choose to close my hand and wrap my fingers around what's in it, it shuts off God's supply to me as well as what I can use to love my neighbor. What's in my hand may be mine, but it will only last for a while before I am left with nothing.

We are going to look at five principles of the open hand in this lesson, drawn from Romans 12:9–16. It is interesting that these principles follow, in Paul's letter to the Rome church, the principle of being a "living sacrifice" in Romans 12:1. Part of living sacrificially unto God is to live with an open hand so that God can give and take and allow us to be a blessing to others.

Julian Huxley was never a follower of Christ. He rejected the Bible, but he did correctly note this: "It doesn't take much of a man to be a Christian, it [just] takes all of him." And Henry Drummond, who was a contemporary of D. L. Moody, said it this way: "The entrance fee to God's kingdom is nothing, but the annual dues are everything." What Drummond said was this: You don't work to become a Christian. But when you become a Christian, then your whole life is caught up in living out the Christian life—and it's not a "walk in the park." Sometimes it's like being in a war, especially when it comes to living with an open hand. Human nature wants to grasp and hold tightly to everything that's in its hand. The Spirit and the flesh are at odds with each other over trusting God with what we have versus what we need versus what others need that we might supply (Galatians 5:16–18).

Following are the five principles of generous (open-handed) living.

# GENEROSITY (ROMANS 12:8)

At the end of Paul's discussion of spiritual gifts, he mentions giving, saying that one who gives should give "with liberality." It seems that people with the gift of giving also have the ability to earn money and accumulate resources that they then gladly distribute to others in need. But whether we have the gift of giving or not, the biblical principle attached to giving is that we should give liberally, or generously. In other words, we should give to others the same way God has given to us.

To give generously means to give with joy, with eagerness, without any ulterior motives, giving purely out of a generous desire to help those who are in need. We find numerous examples of generous giving in Scripture. Barnabas (Acts 4:36–37) comes to mind, he who sold a piece of property he owned and gave the proceeds to the apostles in the earliest days of the church in Jerusalem. The Macedonians, mentioned by Paul in 2 Corinthians 8–9, gave generously out of their own limited resources (8:1–4).

It's easy to think of reasons not to give, isn't it? I often hear people say they're afraid the money won't be used wisely. But that's really not our problem—that's the recipient's problem. Our "problem" is to open our hand and be generous just as God has been generous toward us.

I received a letter once from a grandmother in our church about how she had noticed the sign of life of generous giving in her eight-year-old grandson. His children's ministry group had adopted a group of poor children in one of the Baltic nations in Europe. Each child had a jar in which they were going to save quarters to give toward the adopted children's needs. When the young boy received his five-dollar monthly allowance, he put the entire amount in the jar. When asked why, he replied, "I want the children in [the country] to hear about Jesus. Anyway, I would just buy another toy with the money." Adopting the innocence of children is something to which we adults ought to aspire when it comes to money.

Just as the natural activity for birds is flying and for fish is swimming, so the super-natural activity of human beings ought to be to give. It is the environment into which we were born-again. But like baby birds that fear leaving the nest, some of us desperately hold on to what we have, fearful of launching out into the arena of generous giving. We think we're going to fall to earth or drown, not realizing that giving is what we are called to be and do by God.

## SINCERITY (ROMANS 12:9)

Paul moves on to talk about sincerity, a trait that easily applies to giving. He does so by saying, "Let love be without hypocrisy." Or, as the J. B. Phillips translation of the New Testament says, "Let us have no imitation Christian love."[2]

It's easy to give with insincerity or hypocrisy. The religious leaders in Jesus' day did it, making sure everyone knew how much they put into the temple treasury (Matthew 6:1–4). They were giving for the wrong reason—for themselves, not for God or for others. But insincerity (hypocrisy) is not treated lightly in the New Testament. Peter says we should have "sincere love" (1 Peter 1:22); John wrote that we should love "in truth" (1 John 3:18); and Paul wrote that we should have "a pure heart, from a good conscience, and from sincere faith" (1 Timothy 1:5).

There is no reward from God for giving that is done hypocritically, based on a desire for people to think well of us. God wants us to give out of a sincere faith—a faith that recognizes the generosity of God.

## HUMILITY (ROMANS 12:10)

Someone has said, if you want to give something that no one else ever gives, give preference. That fits perfectly with Paul's words in verse 10: "Be kindly affectionate to one another with brotherly love, in honor giving preference to one another." Giving preference is another sign of a generous spirit. (There are more things we can give than just money!)

In Greek, "giving preference" means to put others in the lead, to let them go before you, to allow them to receive honor before you seek honor for yourself. It definitely takes humility to let others go before oneself. Humility keeps showing up as we study the signs of life! It is an indispensable, nonnegotiable characteristic of those who follow Jesus Christ in sincerity and truth. Pride cannot coexist in the heart with generosity of spirit. Pride grabs position and prestige for self, whereas humility lets it flow to another.

We've studied humility already in this series in connection with Jesus' washing the disciples' feet. Any of us would be willing to wash the feet of Jesus if asked, but how many of us are ready to wash the feet (sacrificially serve) the least of those among us? An openhearted and openhanded person will.

## SYMPATHY (ROMANS 12:13a)

Many times our giving is motivated directly by the needs that people have. As Paul says in verse 13, a sign of sincere and generous love is "distributing to the needs of the saints." There are certainly records in the New Testament of giving that was done on that basis—in particular the relief effort undertaken to give money to the church in Jerusalem by churches in Greece and Macedonia.

Deuteronomy 15:11 is a powerful verse in this regard: "For the poor will never cease from the land; therefore I command you, saying, 'You shall open your hand wide to your brother, to your poor and your needy, in your land.'" It even contains the concept of the open hand! It was a law in Israel that those with an abundance were to open their hands and give to the "poor and needy" in their land.

# HOSPITALITY (ROMANS 12:13b)

The last phrase of verse 13—"given to hospitality"—speaks to one of the most gracious ways to demonstrate open-handed living. And hospitality is not just waiting until someone knocks on our door. Rather, it is reaching out to those in need and inviting them to partake of what the Lord has given us. In your church, there are no doubt people who are going through a difficult time. The simple act of inviting them into your home for a meal, the act of entering into their lives, may be just the bit of encouragement they need to continue trusting the Lord. Yes, you may not know them very well. But what better way to get to know them than to invite them into your home?

First Peter 4:9 says, "Be hospitable to one another without grumbling." If you have ever closed the door after the last guest left your home, turned to your spouse, and said, "Whew! I'm sure glad that's over!"—then you know what Peter is saying. Living with an open hand should not be a burdensome responsibility. It is a privilege, a high calling from God by which we use what He has put into our hands to bless others.

Paul began Romans 12 by beseeching us to present our bodies as "a living sacrifice" to God (verse 1). The first thing that comes to mind with that phrase is the martyrs and missionaries throughout two millennia of church history who have sacrificed their lives for the Lord. Those individuals certainly lived sacrificial lives in the most literal sense of the word.

But Paul exhorts us to be *living* sacrifices—those who live day-to-day in a sacrificial manner for the benefit of Christ and His kingdom. And that certainly means living an open-handed life by which we minister to the needs of others through what God has given to us. Writer Fred Craddock illustrates what this means:

> "True sacrifice will be measured in a thousand small acts of love, not in the martyrs' fire. To give my life for Christ appears glorious. To pour myself out for others . . . to pay the ultimate price of martyrdom — I'll do that. I'm ready, Lord, to go out in a blaze of glory. We think giving our all to the Lord is like taking a $1,000 bill and laying it on the table—"Here's my life, Lord. I'm giving it all." The reality for most of us is that He sends us to the bank with that thousand dollars and asks us to exchange it for quarters. And go through life putting 25 cents here, 50 cents there.

Listen to the neighbor kid's troubles instead of saying, 'Get lost' . . . give a cup of water to a shaky old man who needs help. Usually giving our life to Christ is not glorious." [3]

There's no glory in the unnoticed acts of kindness that we do day in and day out. God hasn't called us, most of us, to give our lives for Him, to be burned at the stake for our faith as martyrs. But He has given us an infinite number of quarters—literal and figurative—that we can spend on others. If you will spend them, He will replace them—if your hand stays open.

Notes:

1. James Stalker, *Imago Christi* (Cincinnati: Cranston & Curts, 1894), 205–206.

2. J. B. Phillips, *The New Testament in Modern English* (Macmillan, 1961).

3. Craig Brian Larson, ed., *Illustrations for Preaching & Teaching: From Leadership Journal* (Grand Rapids: Baker Books, 1993), 200.

1. Read Acts 20:32–35.

   a. How tightly did the apostle Paul hold what was in his hand (or seek to hold what belonged to others)? (verse 33)

   b. Besides himself, whose provision flowed from the apostle's hands? (verse 34)

   c. What was Paul's purpose in earning his own wages rather than depending on the churches for support? (verse 35a)

   d. What point did Paul make about his financial support in 1 Corinthians 9:1–15?

   e. Why do you think Paul was so careful about finances?

   f. In what way(s) do you think it is more blessed to give than to receive? (verse 35)

   g. If Paul had received money from the churches, what blessing would he have missed out on? (verse 34b)

   h. What blessings have you found in your own life from giving to others?

i. Did Jesus say that there was no blessing in receiving? What actually did He say about receiving versus giving? Explain why both giving and receiving are a blessing (but why giving is the greater blessing). (verse 35)

2. Read Matthew 6:1–4.

   a. What did Jesus say about reward from God when "acts of righteousness" are done for the wrong reason? (verse 1)

   b. What do hypocrites do when they give? What is their goal? (verse 2a)

   c. From whom do their rewards come? (verse 2b)

   d. What is the meaning of the "left hand . . . right hand" image in verse 3?

   e. Why does God want our giving to be done in secret? (verse 4a)

   f. Who is secrecy designed to benefit? The giver? The recipient? (verse 4a)

   g. How does this work out practically? Should you give all gifts anonymously? When should they be secret, and when is it okay for the recipient to know who the giver is?

h. What does God do for those who don't advertise their giving for self-promoting purposes? (verse 4b)

3. Read 2 Corinthians 8:1–5.

a. How does Paul describe the Macedonians' generosity? (verse 2)

b. Why were they able to give that way? (verse 1)

c. What does "beyond their ability" mean? (verse 3)

d. How do you know they lived openhanded lives? (verse 5)

---

### DID YOU KNOW?

---

"Poor" is a relative term in the world. According to a 2004 Heritage Foundation report, based on U.S. government census and other reports, the average poor person in America in 2003 (as defined by the government) had a car, air conditioning, a refrigerator, stove, clothes washer and dryer, microwave, two color TV's, cable or satellite TV reception, a VCR or DVD player, and a stereo. His family was not hungry, and he had sufficient funds to meet the family's basic needs. Recognizing that this is an average means that there are many in America who do not have these resources. For example, one-tenth of the poor in America have no telephone, and a third experience problems such as overcrowding, hunger, and no access to medical care.

# OPEN HANDS—LIVING A BLESSED LIFE

### *2 Corinthians 9:6–15*

*In this lesson we study God's Harvest Law—
what it means to sow and reap in the kingdom of God.*

---

**OUTLINE**

Everyone understands the laws of the physical universe—the law of gravity, for example. And only a foolish person would try to ignore them. But there are spiritual laws that are just as irrefutable—the Harvest Law, for example. The wise will acknowledge it and enjoy its benefits.

I. **The Principles of God's Harvest Law**
   A. Investment—We Only Reap if We Sow
   B. Identity—We Reap Only What We Sow
   C. Increase—We Reap More Than We Sow
   D. Interval—We Reap Later Than We Sow

II. **The Products of God's Harvest Law**
   A. We Prosper Spiritually and Financially
   B. We Prove Our Love for God
   C. We Provide for Those in Need
   D. We Provoke Many Thanksgivings to God
   E. We Promote Prayer in Our Behalf
   F. We Purchase Greater Opportunity to Give Again

III. **The Perfect Example of God's Harvest Law**

E xcept for a few intrepid folks through the years who have tried to prove that humans can fly, I don't think many people challenge the law of gravity. We take it as a nonnegotiable law and live accordingly. There is nothing we can do to change it, so we learn to benefit from it and avoid the consequences of breaking it.

Unfortunately, most people (even many Christians) do not take God's spiritual laws as seriously as they do His physical laws. One spiritual law that is stated clearly in Scripture is the Harvest Law—the subject of this lesson. This law is found in its simplest form in Galatians 6:7: "Do not be deceived, God is not mocked; for whatever a man sows, that he will also reap."

Does the law of gravity affect only Christians? Of course not—and neither does the Harvest Law. God's laws are universal and apply to all human beings. I find it very interesting that when Los Angeles was rocked by riots in 1992, when losses of business and property amounted to billions of dollars, all the McDonalds's restaurants were spared by the rioters. Why? They said it was because McDonald's had contributed so much to the lower economic communities—not only food, but jobs as well as financial investments in sports and other inner-city development programs. I believe the Harvest Law was at work: McDonald's gave to the community, and the community spared McDonald's in the riots. They reaped what they had sown.

Though the Harvest Law is stated most succinctly in Galatians 6:7, it is best explained in 2 Corinthians 9:6–15. In this passage we'll discover four principles, six results, and one great example of the Harvest Law at work.

# THE PRINCIPLES OF GOD'S HARVEST LAW

All four principles have to do with the relationships that exist between sowing and reaping.

## Investment—We Only Reap if We Sow

Paul makes an assumption in verse 6: Sowing is taking place. This seems so logical and apparent as to be unnecessary to mention. But many people wonder why they haven't been reaping a harvest in their life, and it may be because they have not been sowing that which they want to reap.

If a farmer wants to reap corn late in the summer, there's only one thing in the world that will make that happen: sowing corn in the spring. It's the Harvest Law, and it cannot be violated. If the farmer saves his kernel of corn or frames it and hangs it in a frame on the wall, he will not have a harvest of corn. If he has a kernel of corn, it will remain a single kernel until it is sown in the ground. Only after it is sown will the kernel become hundreds of new kernels in an ear of corn.

Jesus touched on this principle in John 12:24, saying that unless a grain of wheat falls into the ground and dies "it remains alone." But if it falls into the ground, it "produces much grain." Jesus was talking specifically about death, burial, and resurrection to new life, but the principle is the same. We have to sow in order to reap.

Failure to observe God's Harvest Law may be one reason why wealth brings such little joy to many who have it. Joy comes only from sowing (giving, investing) what God has given in ways that bring returns that benefit others and glorify Him.

## Identity—We Reap Only What We Sow

The principle says that we reap exactly the same kind as we sow. Paul expressed this in Galatians 6:8: "For he who sows to his flesh will of the flesh reap corruption, but he who sows to the Spirit will of the Spirit reap everlasting life."

If the farmer plants corn, he's going to get corn; plants carrots, he'll get carrots, and so on. He cannot expect to get something different in the harvest than what he planted in the sowing. And if I am an angry person, sowing anger into other people's lives, then anger is what I will reap from them. I cannot sow criticism and expect to get understanding, anger and expect to get peace. If we want to have friends, we have to sow friendship (Proverbs 18:24).

## Increase—We Reap More Than We Sow

This principle says we reap more than we sow. Paul says in 2 Corinthians 9:10 that God will "multiply the seed [we] have sown."

Think what the world of agriculture would be like if each fruit or vegetable contained one seed that had to be replanted each year in order to get one more piece of produce. The miraculous nature of God's Harvest Law is that we reap many times more than we sow. When the farmer sows one kernel of corn, he gets a stalk of corn with two or three ears, each of which contain hundreds of kernels. So he harvests hundreds of times what he sowed.

Luke 6:38 is a key verse in this regard: "Give, and it will be given to you: good measure, pressed down, shaken together, and running over will be put into your bosom. For with the same measure that you use, it will be measured back to you." If we sow generously, we are going to reap generously. It's impossible to out-give God.

And please note: This is not a negotiation with God. This is a Harvest Law, a "done deal" to use business terms. Just as the law of gravity is not renegotiated whenever a child kicks a ball into the air, so the Harvest Law is not renegotiated when you give generously to God. Paul uses the words "abound," "abundance," "bountifully," and others in 2 Corinthians 8–9 to show how generously God does His part in the Harvest Law.

And His bounty is realized not just in money; the blessing of God comes in many ways. Whatever we invest—kindness, love, money, ministry—there will be an increase.

## Interval—We Reap Later Than We Sow

Galatians 6:9 says, "in due season we shall reap." *In due season* is the key. There is a season for sowing and a season for reaping, and they are separated by the passage of time.

Suppose a farmer plants his corn in the morning, goes home to have lunch, then goes back in the afternoon to check on the progress of the crop. He complains to his wife that nothing is happening—the corn is not growing. That's a comical example, of course; yet in the spiritual world, that's how we act at times.

In the world of agriculture, who sets the time gap between sowing and reaping? Nature does, or the genetic instructions contained in each individual seed. In the spiritual realm, who controls the timetable? God does, of course. Just as every seed has its own timetable, so every spiritual act has its own gap between sowing and reaping as worked out by God.

Here's how God's timetable worked out in my father's life. In 1953, he was called to be president of Cedarville College, a small, struggling Christian college in Ohio. The school had ninety students, substandard facilities, and no money. But he poured himself into that school for fifty years—twenty-five as president and twenty-five as chancellor. In the early years, my mother and father did a lot of sowing into Cedarville College and very little reaping.

The school grew steadily under my father's administration (today it is Cedarville University with more than 3,000 students). Near the end of his ministry, he was still traveling and speaking and keeping up an active schedule on behalf of the college; and I asked him why he didn't slow down and enjoy a bit of rest. He told me how he loved to travel around and see the work that former students were doing for Christ, both in ministry and in secular fields. He said, "I am clipping coupons off of a lifetime of investment."

It took many years for my father to reap the harvest of his years of intensive sowing into a small Christian college. But in due time, he began to see the fruit of his labors. Fifty years seems like a long time, but some harvests take more time than others. Our responsibility is to be faithful to sow; God's is to be faithful to bring the harvest.

# THE PRODUCTS OF GOD'S HARVEST LAW

As the farmer reaps produce (fruits, vegetables, grains) from his sowing, so we reap products from ours.

## We Prosper Spiritually and Financially
### (2 Corinthians 9:10)

God "[supplies] and [multiplies] the seed you have sown and [increases] the fruits of your righteousness." As we give to the Lord financially, He multiplies what we have. This is not just a promise for our financial welfare but for our spiritual welfare as well: God promises to increase the "fruits of [our] righteousness." As we sow financially into the kingdom of God, we are blessed with increasing spiritual maturity as well as having our financial needs met.

## We Prove Our Love for God (2 Corinthians 9:13)

Paul says that the generosity of the Corinthian believers will cause people to "glorify God" as they see the sacrifice of those who confess the Gospel of Jesus Christ. It's one thing to say we love Christ, but it's another to give sacrificially in His name.

Try this next Christmas: Instead of demonstrating your love for your spouse by giving him or her a wonderful gift, just say, "You know I love you—I tell you all the time that I do. I hope you have a merry Christmas!" If you're out of the doghouse by next Christmas, I'd be surprised! Talk doesn't satisfy like actions. And when we demonstrate our love for God by sowing sacrificially, we bring glory to Him by showing our love for Him.

## We Provide for Those in Need (2 Corinthians 9:12)

When the Corinthians gave toward the needs of the church in Jerusalem, their gifts supplied "the needs of the saints." And that's what our gifts to God do, directly or indirectly, today all over the world. If you give to your local church, your gifts go to provide for ministries to children, young people, and adults. Either through your church or through mission agencies, your gifts send and support missionaries all over the world. And other gifts go directly to assist individuals or families who are in crisis and have significant needs. God puts money into our hands so that we can channel those funds in a multitude of directions to meet the needs of people—all in the name of Christ and for the sake of the Gospel.

## We Provoke Many Thanksgivings to God
### (2 Corinthians 9:11, 12, 15)

When we give financially for the sake of the Gospel, we begin a chain reaction of thanks that redound to God from whom all good and perfect gifts flow (James 1:17).

When we give our money on Sunday at church, part of it goes to a mission agency. That mission agency then sends support funds to their missionaries. Those missionaries use some of those funds to meet spiritual and material needs of those to whom they are ministering. And all along that chain of events, people are giving thanks to God. You thank Him for His provision, the church leaders do, the mission leaders do, the missionaries do, and those to whom they minister do. So your single gift results in a multitude of thanks being given to God.

## We Promote Prayer in Our Behalf
### (2 Corinthians 9:14)

Those who are blessed by our giving pray to God for us, thanking Him for His grace at work in our lives and praying that our needs will be met. This is what those in Jerusalem did for the Corinthians and Macedonians who contributed to their needs. There are people all over the world who pray for our church, and for your church, because of the ministry our churches are having in their lives. And those ministries are the result of our gifts which we sow faithfully.

## We Purchase Greater Opportunity to Give Again (2 Corinthians 9:8)

Verse 8 says that we, from our sowing, will "have an abundance for every good work." When we give, God blesses us. And when He blesses us, we have adequate supply to give again. And the sowing and reaping cycle continues to repeat itself. God does not bless us so we can hoard His blessing for ourselves, but so we can pass on the blessing to others. God blesses us to be a blessing; and as long as we continue to sow, the cycle of blessing will continue. But the cycle of blessing can be broken the day we decide to clasp our fingers tightly around what God has given us. Not only does the sowing stop, but the reaping as well.

## THE PERFECT EXAMPLE OF GOD'S HARVEST LAW (2 CORINTHIANS 9:15)

Hebrews 2:10 says that God is going to bring "many sons to glory." How did He do that? By sowing His one and only Son into this world where He died and was raised to new life. Like a single seed sown into the ground that results in many seeds being harvested, Jesus Christ became "the firstborn among many brothers" (Romans 8:29). God's own practice of the Harvest Law becomes a pattern for us to follow in our lives: sowing and reaping for eternal profit.

Are your hands open, sharing what God has given you, sowing into the work of Christ? If so you are, or will be, reaping the harvest, living a blessed life. If your hands are closed, I encourage you to get in step with God's irrefutable Harvest Law for your good, the good of others, and His glory.

1. Read Galatians 6:7–10.

   a. If a person does not believe his life will have consequences tied to his actions, we would say he is _____ . (verse 7a)

   b. Why is "mocking" the term that is used here?

   c. What does the word "whatever" suggest? How all-inclusive is the Harvest Law?

   d. What does the person who sows to his flesh reap? (verse 8a) How would you define this term? What are its temporal and eternal ramifications?

   e. What will the person reap who sows to the Spirit? (verse 8b) When does "everlasting life" begin?

   f. What is the biggest temptation when sowing "to the Spirit"? (verse 9)

   g. What would be an example of losing heart, say, when sowing financially to the Lord?

   h. Have you ever lost heart when sowing? Why? What was the result? What harvest did you miss out on by losing heart?

i. What degree of certainty is attached to the words "we shall reap"? How important is the little word "if" in this equation? (verse 9)

j. What is the longest "due season" you have endured before reaping the harvest from your sowing? (verse 9)

k. List as many "opportunities" to "do good" as you can think of that might occur in an average week of your life. (verse 10)

l. List as many categories of people as you think might be included in the word "all." (verse 10)

m. Cite an example of the Harvest Law in your life—how you sowed and what you reaped.

2. Read Matthew 19:21–30.

a. What is the context of these verses as summarized in verses 21–23?

b. How did Peter contrast what he and the disciples had done compared to what the man had been unwilling to do? (verses 22, 27)

c. How would you describe what the disciples had done in terms of sowing? What had they sowed? (verse 27)

d. What "reaping" question did Peter ask? (verse 27b)


e. Jesus said the disciples would reap their rewards in three ways. (verses 28–29) What were they?


- (verse 28) They would become _____ over Israel.


- (verse 29) They would receive a _____ .


- (verse 29) They would inherit _____

    _____ .


3  What harvest are you expecting from the sowing you have done for the Lord?


---

**DID YOU KNOW?**

---

One person who lived his life (unknowingly) in light of God's Harvest Law was the American inventor, designer, and architect Buckminster Fuller (d. 1983). Fuller is best known for his invention of the geodesic dome structure. When Fuller received royalty checks for his inventions, he would often pay his employees and the expenses of his company, and give the rest away. He would frequently spend his own money down to the last penny. His philosophy was, "If you devote your time and attention to the highest advantage of others, the universe will support you always and only in the nick of time." It wasn't "the universe" that was supporting him—it was God through the operation of the Harvest Law.

# OUTSTRETCHED ARMS— LIVING A COMPASSIONATE LIFE

### *Luke 10:25–37*

*In this lesson we learn what it means to love your neighbor.*

---

### OUTLINE

---

Everybody knows who their neighbors are. They're the people who live next door, around the corner, or across the street. But a story Jesus told leads to a different definition of neighbor. Our neighbor is anyone who has a need which we are able to meet—with love and compassion.

I. **To the Lawyer, Love Was Just a Subject to Explore**

II. **To the Thieves, Love Was a Soul to Exploit**

III. **To the Priest, Love Was a Situation to Evade**

IV. **To the Levite, Love Was Someone to Examine**

V. **To the Samaritan, Love Was a Sympathy to Express**
   A. His Love Was Displayed by Compassion
   B. His Love Was Demonstrated by Contact
   C. His Love Was Delivered With Care
   D. His Love Was Documented by Cost

VI. **To the Christian, Love Is Something to Demonstrate**
   A. The Secret to Loving Is Not Found in Religion
   B. The Secret to Loving Is Not Found in Rules
   C. The Secret to Loving Is Found in a Relationship

I n the book *Chicken Soup for the Christian Family Soul*, Rebecca Pippert tells the story of Bill.

Bill was a college student with long hair who mostly wore T-shirts and jeans with holes in them. But he had become a Christian. One Sunday Bill decided to visit the church across the street from the college campus. When he walked in on that Sunday morning, the church was packed; he didn't see a single empty seat. So he walked down the center aisle and sat down on the carpet in front of the pulpit.

This was highly unorthodox behavior in this very formal church, and no one quite knew what to make of Bill and his choice of seats. But from near the back of the church, an elderly deacon began making his way toward the front of the church, walking slowly with his cane. Surely, most folks thought, this respected deacon would correct Bill's behavior. But when the deacon got to the front of the church, to everyone's surprise, he lowered himself on his stiff knees to the carpet and sat right next to Bill.

The pastor had stopped speaking while this took place, but then he uttered these words: "What I am about to preach, you will never remember; but what you have just seen, you will never forget." [1]

You may forget most of what is in this chapter in the days ahead, but I hope you don't forget the image that story represents—and the story Jesus told that illustrates the same point: loving one's neighbor. The story of the good Samaritan is one of Jesus' most loved and most widely known stories. And it illustrates the same point as the story you just read: Our love for God is displayed by how well we love others.

In Jesus' story of the good Samaritan, we will meet four categories of people. You will likely identify with one of the four—and hopefully it will be the last one: the good Samaritan.

# TO THE LAWYER, LOVE WAS JUST A SUBJECT TO EXPLORE (LUKE 10:25–29)

The story begins with a lawyer who asked what was, on the surface, a legitimate question about gaining eternal life. But Luke tells us the lawyer had an ulterior motive: He was testing Jesus (verse 25). He took a sincere topic and framed it with an insincere question.

Religious leaders of Jesus' day (as leaders in every generation do; Acts 17:21) loved to discuss the fine points of religion and social matters. They didn't do much about them, but they loved to argue about them. And this lawyer was trying to engage Jesus in such a debate—on the fine points of Jewish law concerning eternal life.

The lawyer knew the Old Testament, quoting exactly from Deuteronomy 6:5 and Leviticus 19:18. When he asked Jesus, "And who is my neighbor?" he betrayed the fact that he had not loved his neighbor. If he was in the practice of loving his neighbor, he would know whom it was he loved. He was avoiding the issue of love by trying to focus on the "legal" definition of "neighbor." Instead of answering the lawyer's question in verse 29, Jesus told him a story.

# TO THE THIEVES, LOVE WAS A SOUL TO EXPLOIT (LUKE 10:30)

The story was about a man who went from Jerusalem to Jericho and was attacked on the way by thieves. For these thieves, a stranger was definitely not a neighbor; people were just souls to exploit for their own gain.

The road from Jerusalem to Jericho was a perfect place for thieves to ambush travelers. And the thieves who attacked the traveler in Jesus' story stole his clothes and possessions, beat him, and left him for dead. Jesus was painting a picture for the lawyer to see in his mind, a picture of who a neighbor is and what love in action looks like.

# TO THE PRIEST, LOVE WAS A SITUATION TO EVADE (LUKE 10:31)

The first person to come along and see the traveler lying half-dead by the side of the road was a priest. But for the priest, it was a situation to evade rather than an opportunity to show real love.

This priest probably lived in Jericho and was going to Jerusalem to perform his duty in the temple in service to God. But he couldn't be inconvenienced by a dying man on the road. Indeed, he moved to the other side of the road as he walked past. Had the priest examined the man and discovered he was dead, he would have become ceremonially unclean for seven days, disqualifying him from serving in the temple. It was a chance he was unwilling to take. He chose temple service above the life of a suffering human being.

# To the Levite, Love Was Someone to Examine (Luke 10:32)

The second person to come along was a Levite. He slowed down and looked at the man but moved to the other side of the road and kept walking. The wounded man represented a point of curiosity but not an opportunity for love.

If the priest was the equivalent of a pastor, the Levite was like a worship leader, a minister in the temple service. He had the required knowledge to know that it was his duty to love his neighbor; but for whatever reason, he chose not to.

The priest and the Levite both demonstrate that religious work doesn't make one religious, that religious isn't the same as righteous. They were on their way to serve God but invalidated their service by failing to serve their fellow man.

# To the Samaritan, Love Was a Sympathy to Express (Luke 10:33-37)

The third person to come along the road was the hero of the story—a Samaritan, a man despised by the Jews. He saw the wounded traveler as an opportunity to express love; he saw the man as his neighbor.

Of all the people involved in this story—a Jewish lawyer, priest, and Levite, and a Samaritan—the Levite would be the least likely to help the Jewish traveler from a cultural perspective. The lawyer listening to this story must have flinched at the idea of the Samaritan being the hero.

We can note four things about the Samaritan's response to his neighbor, the wounded Jewish traveler.

## His Love Was Displayed by Compassion
### (Luke 10:33)

Jesus says in His story that when the Samaritan encountered the wounded traveler, "he had compassion" on him (verse 33). All three of the men who came by saw the wounded man, but only one saw him with eyes of compassion. It is possible for all of us to be guilty of seeing without compassion.

I had heard about the AIDS tragedy that has afflicted so much of Africa. I had seen pictures, TV programs, and heard missionaries talk about it. But until I went there, the country in Africa with the highest rate of AIDS in all of Africa, I didn't really know what it was like. I had seen the tragedy; but after I went to Africa personally, I saw it differently. I saw it with compassion. Jesus calls us to leave our comfort zones and go to uncomfortable places in order that our eyes might be opened to the needs of our neighbors.

## His Love Was Demonstrated by Contact (Luke 10:34)

The Samaritan reached out with his hands and demonstrated his compassion and love. He cleaned and bandaged the traveler's wounds, set him upon his own donkey, and took him to an inn so he could rest and begin to recover. He risked his own life to help a man he didn't know. After all, the thieves might have been in hiding, waiting for someone to stop and help the man. He demonstrated his compassion by investing himself in the needs of the stranger.

## His Love Was Delivered With Care (Luke 10:37)

The lawyer himself is the one who observed the care with which the Samaritan treated the traveler: "He . . . showed mercy on him" (verse 37). It was the Samaritan's acts of kindness that stood out to the lawyer in contrast to the lack of kindness by the priest and the Levite. It was obvious who was the most caring among the three.

## His Love Was Documented by Cost (Luke 10:35)

The Samaritan took money out of his own pocket and paid for the wounded man to stay in an inn. There is always a price when we exercise love. God so loved the world, and it cost Him the suffering and death of His own Son. The Samaritan paid with his time, his money, his disrupted schedule, his energy for letting the wounded man ride on his donkey while he himself walked, his reputation for having helped a Jew, and the risk of being attacked while helping the traveler.

The Christian life, if it is going to be lived in love, is going to cost. Someone has said that it doesn't cost anything to become a Christian, but it costs everything to be a Christian. Love without sacrifice is probably not genuine love at all.

When Jesus finished His story, He asked the lawyer. "So which of these three do you think was neighbor to him who fell among the thieves?" (verse 36). And the lawyer answered correctly: "He who showed mercy on him" (verse 37). And Jesus told him to "Go and do likewise" (verse 37).

It's not enough to get the right answer—to know compassion and mercy when you see it. If we are going to follow Jesus, we have to get involved. We have to leave our comfort zone and love our neighbor in a hands-on way that makes a difference.

# To the Christian, Love Is Something to Demonstrate

I'll close this lesson by giving you three secrets about the kind of love that has compassion on a neighbor.

## The Secret to Loving Is Not Found in Religion

You don't become a loving person by becoming a religious person or by going to church. It's been said that sitting in church doesn't make you a real Christian any more than sitting in a garage makes you a car. There are lots of unloving people in churches today.

The first three characters in Jesus' story were all religious: The lawyer, the priest, and the Levite. The lawyer knew the Mosaic law inside and out; the priest was a religious leader; the Levite was a trained worshipper. But none of them were loving people. They were more concerned about their own religiosity than they were about the well-being of their neighbor. And they ought to serve as a warning to all Christians. We are not followers of Jesus because we take up a seat in a particular building on Sunday mornings. We are followers of Jesus if we hear His Word and obey it, if we actually express the love of God toward those who need His love in this world.

## The Secret to Loving Is Not Found in Rules

When Jesus asked the lawyer what the law said about eternal life, he knew to love God and to love his neighbor. He knew what the Bible said. He just didn't want to put it into practice.

At the beginning, the lawyer asked, "And who is my neighbor?" (verse 29). But at the end of the story, Jesus changed the question and said, "Who acted like a neighbor?" (paraphrase). Instead of focusing on who qualified as the lawyer's neighbor, Jesus focused on the kind of person the neighbor should be. A person like the Samaritan doesn't perform a litmus test to determine who is his neighbor. He's the kind of person, in the words of one of my seminary professors, Haddon Robinson, who helps anyone who has a need whose need he is able to meet.

Jesus' point is not, "Who qualifies to be loved." Rather, it is, "Who qualifies as a loving person?" It is not defining our neighbor that makes us loving, it is loving whoever needs our help that qualifies us as a loving neighbor. Jesus expanded the boundaries of our neighborhood to the whole world by the telling of this story.

## The Secret to Loving Is Found in a Relationship

Many older Bible commentators have compared the Samaritan's acts of kindness to what God has done for mankind in Christ Jesus. Just like the traveler, we lie broken beside the road of life, unable to help ourselves, and robbed by sin and Satan of God's gifts of life and abundance. But God came down in Jesus Christ and covered our nakedness, bound our wounds, and poured upon us the ointment of His Spirit. He put us in a place of shelter and rest and is paying the expense of our full recovery. And like the good Samaritan, Christ promised to return and ensure our full recovery!

Because Jesus has been the "good Samaritan" to us, we can be a loving neighbor to those who are in need whom we encounter in life. Jesus calls us to leave our security, our schedules, and our safety, and stop along our way to minister to those who need our help. We are not called to be religious or to follow a system of rules. But we are called to live our lives, following in the footsteps of the One who loved us enough to meet every need we have.

We have noted previously in these lessons that you and I may be the only picture of Jesus that some people ever see. If they see religion and rules, they won't be seeing Him. But if they see love that comes from a relationship with God—love that reaches out to anyone and everyone to meet their needs—they will see the real Jesus. When they see a true neighbor, they will see the Jesus who died for them.

### Note:

1. Rebecca Manley Pippert, "A Guy Named Bill" in *Chicken Soup for the Christian Family Soul*, ed. Jack Canfield and Mark Victor Hansen, (Deerfield Beach: Health Communications, Inc., 2000), 36. http://www.chickensoup.com/stories/christian_fam/bill.html.

## APPLICATION

1. Read Matthew 9:35–38.

   a. What was the scope of Jesus' ministry as described in verse 35a?

   b. What were Jesus' activities in these places? (verse 35b)

   c. What was Jesus' emotional response to the people He encountered? (verse 36)

   d. Translate "weary and scattered, like sheep having no shepherd" into your own words. What was it about the people that prompted compassion from Jesus? (verse 36)

   e. What were the "boundaries" of Jesus' neighborhood based on these verses? Whom did He consider His neighbors?

   f. What was the ethnicity of the woman Jesus ministered to in John 4:1–26?

   g. How about the woman in Matthew 15:22? What was Jesus' initial response to her? (verse 24) How did He ultimately respond to her? (verse 28)

   h. What was the social condition of the men Jesus ministered to in Luke 17:11–19?

i. What about the woman to whom Jesus ministered in Luke 7:36–39?


j. What do you conclude about whom Jesus considered to be His neighbors?


2. Read 1 Corinthians 13:1–13.

a. In what way do verses 1–3 describe the lawyer, priest, and Levite in the context of the Good Samaritan story?

b. Why is love the primary evidence of a heart that truly "sees" the needs of people? (verse 13)


c. Of all the actions characteristic of love in verses 4–8a, which of these would be the hardest to exercise toward a perfect stranger?


d. How does true love from a stranger make a needy person feel?


e. How do young people often act toward those not in their circle or clique? (verse 11a) Why is love for one's neighbor a sign of spiritual maturity (putting away childish things)? (verse 11b)


3. What groups of people do you find yourself not "seeing" with eyes of compassion when you encounter them?

a. Why is it easy to act pharisaical (judgmental) toward those in need?

b. How do Romans 5:8 and 10 illustrate how God overcame what might be a natural response to unlovely persons?

c. What (or who) should we "see" when we look at those in need?

4. How did the lawyer with whom Jesus conversed violate the principle in James 1:22?

a. What was his spiritual condition? (verse 22b)

b. What is the condition of the man who not only hears (knows) the Word but also does it? (verse 25b)

c. What part of the Old Testament did the lawyer know but fail to practice? (Leviticus 19:18b)

---

### DID YOU KNOW?

---

Who were the Samaritans, and why did they and the Jews despise one another? When the Assyrians invaded northern Israel (Samaria) in 721 B.C., a large part of the Jewish population was carried off into exile. The Assyrians moved in a large population of their own people to populate the region, and they intermarried with the Jewish remnant left in the land (contrary to Jewish law). A mixed religion developed. When the Jews from Judah and Jerusalem returned from exile in Babylon, the "Samaritans" counted themselves worthy of having a part in the rebuilding of Jerusalem and the temple. But the returning Jews would have none of it, and a permanent schism developed. Many Samaritans were won to Christ in the revival documented in Acts 8.

# OUTSTRETCHED ARMS— LIVING A LIFE OF COMMUNITY

## *1 Peter 3:8*

*In this lesson we learn how the church becomes a community of faith.*

### OUTLINE

When bad things happen in this world, people look for the presence of God. The way God designed His presence to be known is through a community of faith called the church. When God's people live like the family they are called to be, they reveal the presence of the Father.

I. **Community Requires Unity**

II. **Community Reacts With Sympathy**

III. **Community Responds Like Family**

IV. **Community Reaches Out in Sincerity**

V. **Community Reinforces Humility**

I n his book *Reaching for the Invisible God,* author Philip Yancey tells about a man he met who asked Yancey about another of his books, *Where Is God When It Hurts?* The man said he didn't have time to read the book and wondered if Yancey could summarize it for him in a sentence or two. After a moment, Yancey replied, "I suppose I'd have to answer your question with another question: Where is the church when it hurts?"

In other words, the church is God's presence on earth. If the church is doing its job to care for those who hurt, then nobody will ask, "Where is God?" When the world sees those who profess to be God's people taking care of the hurting people in this world, they will know that God is there. It's only when the church fails to represent God adequately that people wonder why God hasn't shown up.

The first word in 1 Peter 3:8 is "finally"—and it is appropriate for our final lesson in this study guide on signs of spiritual life. Peter, prior to verse 8, has been talking about how to get along in the body of Christ—husbands and wives, for example. But then he addresses everyone: "Finally, all of you . . ." (verse 8). He has some principles that help the church live together as the community of believers it is intended to be: "Be of one mind, having compassion for one another; love as brothers, be tenderhearted, be courteous."

Eugene Peterson, author of *The Message* paraphrase of the New Testament, translates verse 8 this way: "Summing up: Be agreeable, be sympathetic, be loving, be compassionate, be humble." Five "simple" things which, if the church practices them, will result not only in people getting along (caring for one another) but in those in the world recognizing that God is in our midst.

# COMMUNITY REQUIRES UNITY

Peter says to "be of one mind," a perfect description of unity. It's easy to see that "unity" is at the heart of "community." In fact, it's impossible to have community without unity. Whether in a family, small group, a church, a business, or a government, unity is a requirement for community. Unity provides focus, purpose, and direction. Even when there are disagreements, unity of focus keeps the community together.

In the church, our focus is Jesus Christ; our unity comes from our common commitment to Him. It stands to reason that if all Christians are committed to the person of Christ, all Christians will then be committed to one another. Unfortunately, this unity doesn't manifest itself as consistently today as it did in the early church. Acts 2:46 says the church "continued daily with one accord." And Acts 4:32 says the believers "were of one heart and one soul." The rapid growth of the early church bears witness to their common focus and powerful community.

Unity is not uniformity. We don't all have to dress, speak, and act identically as if we were clones. Nor is unity unanimity—everyone saying exactly the same thing with no one doing any independent or creative thinking. Instead, unity means that all believers share a common love for and obedience and submission to Jesus Christ and His Word. When we disagree, we turn to Him. We submit ourselves to His leading to solve problems. He is the Lord of the church and Lord of our lives.

Unity means we don't focus on *what* we know but *Who* we know. We can have different views and preferences on methods and means, but we are united around the single unifying purpose of the church: fulfilling the Lord's commands.

## COMMUNITY REACTS WITH SYMPATHY

Peter's next admonition is to have "compassion for one another" (verse 8). The word for compassion in the Greek language is *sumpathes*, from which we get our word "sympathy." A community that lives effectively together is one that lives sympathetically— with compassion for one another.

Our English word "compassion" consists of com + passion, which means "with suffering." In other words, when we have compassion, it means we suffer with the other person; we identify with his sufferings or his pain. Romans 12:15 says it best: We "weep with those who weep."

I read once about sheep farmers in New Mexico who were losing lambs in the freezing cold weather. The sheep would be in the pasture, and the adult sheep would not recognize how cold it was getting because of their thick wool coats. They couldn't recognize that their lambs were freezing to death because they hadn't yet grown heavy fleece to protect them. So the sheep farmers shaved the top of the ewes' heads so they could feel when the temperature was dropping and would head for shelter with the lambs trailing behind.

Sometimes we get so immune to the suffering and needs of people around us that God has to "shave the top of our heads." He may send a time of suffering or concern into our own lives so we get shocked back into reality and start seeing the suffering of those around us and participating in their lives. There's nothing like suffering to make us start seeing the suffering that is all around us.

We are blessed to live in a culture devoid of some of the suffering that people in other cultures live with on a daily basis. It's easy for us to live insulated lives from the house to the garage to the car to the parking garage to the office and back home again without interfacing with very many people at all. It's hard to develop and express sympathy and compassion in that kind of lifestyle.

In the book I mentioned earlier by Philip Yancey, *Reaching for the Invisible God*, he shares a story about the power of compassion. A friend of his went through a period of dark depression and ended up in an institution where he tried three times to take his life. Yancey spent several years trying to be of help and encouragement to his friend, feeling that he was accomplishing little. He finally stopped offering advice and decided just to "be there": "And I simply made myself available as much as I could. Eventually my friend experienced a healing that brought him back to sanity; and he said to me one day, 'You were God to me. I had no contact with God the Father; He seemed vacant, withdrawn. But I kept believing in God because of you.'"

Yancey said, "I wanted to shove him away, to refute him, for I knew who I am and how far that is from God. As I listened, though, I realized the profound meaning behind Paul's phrase, 'the body of Christ.' For whatever reason, God had chosen me and a few other 'clay vessels' through which He poured His own presence. And we make this journey not alone; we make this journey, rather, joined to one another." [1]

That is a wonderful example of how community is strengthened through sympathy, through sharing in the sufferings of one another. It is only as we enter into one another's lives that we will be able to build up the body of Christ by strengthening each other.

# COMMUNITY RESPONDS LIKE FAMILY

Loving one another within the body of Christ is a high priority for Peter. Three times in this letter—here and in 1:22 and 2:17—Peter admonishes the church to "love as brothers," to love like a family loves.

More than 200 times, the New Testament uses the term "brothers" to refer to the community of faith. Even though we have disagreements, we are to continue loving one another with a family-like devotion. We can travel anywhere in the world and meet fellow-Christians and feel just like we are part of a huge, worldwide family. It's a wonderful thing to be a Christian and know that we have brothers and sisters all over the world who are part of our spiritual family.

# COMMUNITY REACHES OUT IN SINCERITY

Peter's fourth admonition is that we be "tenderhearted" toward one another—a word echoed by Paul in Ephesians 4:32.

The opposite of tenderhearted is hardhearted—an uncaring person who fights to gain every advantage for himself in life regardless of what it costs others or how it affects their lives. The world tells us that we will get trampled and left behind if we are tenderhearted. For Christians, "tenderhearted" means to have a heart like Jesus Christ's—a heart that can be moved and broken in the presence of another's pain or suffering.

Joanna Siebert wrote a letter to a church magazine some years ago in which she told a story about tenderheartedness that illustrates the idea beautifully.

> Today I visited an eight-year-old girl who was dying of cancer. Her body was disfigured by her disease and its treatment, and she was almost in constant pain. As I entered the room, I was overcome almost immediately by her suffering—which was so unjust and so unfair and so unreasonable, my heart was broken. But even more over-powering, however, was the presence of her grandmother who was lying in bed with her, with her huge body embracing this precious, inhuman suffering.

> I stood in awe for I knew I was on holy ground... I will never forget the great, gentle arms and body of this grandmother. She never spoke while I was there. She was holding and participating in suffering that she could not relieve, and somehow her silent presence was relieving the suffering. No words could express the magnitude of her love.[2]

That's what it means to be tenderhearted—to have hearts that are moved to embrace the suffering and needs of another person. When Lazarus died, Jesus wept (John 11:35). When he looked down on the city of Jerusalem, He agonized over her lost state (Matthew 23:37). If we want to be tenderhearted, we have to see the heart of Jesus. Then we can know what it means to enter into the lives of others with whatever we have to share and offer.

When our church started a program of small groups years ago, the plan was for each group leader to have an apprentice who, after one year, would take part of the group out to start another group. That was my idea, and it was a complete FAILURE! Asking people to break up their family after a year of developing tender hearts toward one another made me look like a home wrecker. So we developed other strategies for starting new groups. But I was delighted to see that people were bonding at the heart level— getting intimately involved in each others' lives.

## COMMUNITY REINFORCES HUMILITY

Peter's last admonition is to "be courteous" to one another. In truth, that's not the best translation of the Greek word. Most modern Bible translations have "humility" or "be humble" as the admonition. Granted, courtesy requires humility. But in our modern English, "humility" is a better representation of the original language.

When you live in community, in a family, you don't always get your own way. It takes humility to yield to another person, to give up your point of view, to be flexible, to compromise. I've been to pastor's conferences where the participants were divided into small groups for discussion. Five or six strong-willed pastor/leaders in a discussion group is not a model of the kind of humility it takes to flex and compromise and build community! But that's what we have to do in the church if we expect to manifest the presence of God in the world via a unified community.

There's a story I heard that illustrates all five of the principles Peter exhorts us to have in our lives: unity, sympathy, family, sincerity, and humility. It took place in Brooklyn, New York, at a school for mildly disabled and mentally challenged children. It was told by the father of one of the students at the school, a young boy named Shya.

Shya and his father were walking past a park where a pickup baseball game was in progress. Shya asked his dad if he thought the boys would let him play. With hesitancy, the father asked one of the boys if Shya could join the game and the young man said he could. The game was in the eighth inning, but he promised to try to get Shya up to bat in the ninth inning. They gave him a glove and sent him to the outfield.

In the last inning, Shya's team was behind by three runs with two outs and the bases loaded—and it was Shya's turn to bat. One of the other boys came up and helped Shya hold the bat, and the opposing pitcher moved in closer and lobbed an easy pitch in. Shya and his helper swung and dribbled a soft hit back to the pitcher. Everyone screamed for Shya to run to first base. The pitcher could easily have thrown him out, but he threw the ball over the first baseman's head—so Shya ran for second. The opposing players kept throwing the ball far off the mark so Shya could keep running until he made it home, scoring the winning run!

The players from both teams crowded around and hoisted Shya onto their shoulders, celebrating a once-in-a-lifetime victory for a kid who had never had such a thrill—who had never been part of such a community.[3]

That's what community—that's what church—is all about. My prayer is that this study guide will encourage you to help your church become that part of a community—the presence of Christ in the world. The world is looking for "signs of life" in us—and the life of Jesus is the greatest sign of them all.

Notes:

1. Philip Yancey, *Reaching for the Invisible God* (Grand Rapids: Zondervan, 2000), 170.

2. Story told by Leonard Sweet in *Postmodern Pilgrims* (Nashville: Broadman & Publishers, 2000), 16.

3. John Ortberg, "Relationships You've Always Wanted, Part 3: The Relatives Are Coming," Willow Creek Association.

## APPLICATION

1. Read 1 Corinthians 12:20–26.

   a. What is Paul's practical goal for what he writes in verses 20–25a? (verse 25b)

   b. What happens to a community of believers if verse 21 is the norm? What are the subtle ways these statements can be made in the church?

   c. Why are "weaker" members of the body "necessary" and deserving of "greater honor"? (verses 22–23)

   d. Why can we say that unity is at the heart of Paul's writings about the lesser members of the body? (verse 25a)

   e. By what two corporate actions can the body of Christ display its community? (verse 26)

   f. When was the last time you rejoiced (not just laughed) with another believer over his or her honor or success?

g. When was the last time you suffered with another believer in his or her time of suffering?

h. What do those experiences do for you? What do they add to your life as the one identifying with another?

2. Read 2 Corinthians 1:3–4.

a. As best you can, explain what "Father of mercies" and "God of all comfort" mean? (verse 3)

b. Besides easing our own pain, for what other reason does God comfort us in our affliction? (verse 4)

c. If a person says, "I really don't know how to help others," what can he use as a model of comfort? (verse 4)

d. How are you comforted by God?

e. What is the best way, generally speaking, you have found to comfort other people?

f. What have you found is least helpful when it comes to comforting others?

3. Read Job 2:11–13.

a. Do you wait to be asked before offering comfort to others? Why or why not?

b. How did Job's friends conclude they should go and comfort Job? (verse 11)

c. What evidence is there that they truly sympathized with Job over his condition? (verse 12)

d. What did they do for the first week they were with Job? (verse 13)

e. What does the text offer as the reason for their silence? (verse 13b)

f. Why is silence better than speaking when someone is suffering?

g. What does a person say nonverbally by not speaking, by just being there?

4. How does Philippians 2:4 serve as a good summary for this lesson's message on community?

---

## DID YOU KNOW?

When Peter wrote that believers should "love as brothers," he used a single word to express that idea: *philadelphos*— love of one's brother. *Philadelphos* is a compound noun made of two other Greek words: *philos* means "beloved, dear, friendly," and *adelphos* means "brother." So *philadelphos* means "beloved or dear brother." Spoken as a verb, it means to love with a brotherly love as one would love a family member. *Philadelphos* is obviously the source for the name of America's "City of Brotherly Love," Philadelphia, Pennsylvania. First Peter 3:8 is the only place *philadelphos* is used in the New Testament, although other similar forms with the same idea occur (Romans 12:10; 1 Thessalonians 4:9; Hebrews 13:1).

# ADDITIONAL RESOURCES
## BY DR. DAVID JEREMIAH

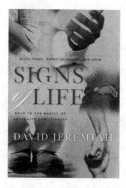

### Signs of Life

In the best-selling book, *Signs of Life,* Dr. David Jeremiah presents five signs of spiritual life every believer should use as a measure of the impact he or she is making for Christ in the world. In this important book you will learn how the world recognizes us as God's ambassadors. Learn about the signs that will advertise your faith—personal imprints that can impact souls for eternity and help you become a person of influence who radiates relevancy, authenticity, generosity, and compassion every day—just like Jesus did.

### Heroes of the Faith in God's Hall of Fame

Where would you go to find a list of modern heroes? In this series you will discover the list of God's heroes. Each person in God's Hall of Fame was chosen for only one reason—their great faith. What Dr. Jeremiah reveals about the lives of God's heroes will encourage you to exercise heroic faith. The doors to the Hall of Faith are still open, and you could become the next hero in God's eyes!